THE CURIOUS
BARTENDER'S
GUIDE TO
MALT, BOURBON & RYE
WHISKIES

THE CURIOUS

BARTENDER'S

GUIDE

TO

MALT, BOURBON & RYE

WHISKIES

TRISTAN STEPHENSON

WITH PHOTOGRAPHY BY ADDIE CHINN

RYLAND PETERS & SMALL
LONDON • NEW YORK

Designers Geoff Borin, Paul Stradling
Editors Nathan Joyce and Julia Charles
Head of Production Patricia Harrington
Art Director Leslie Harrington
Editorial Director Julia Charles
Publisher Cindy Richards

Prop Stylist Sarianne Plaisant
Indexer Hilary Bird

Originally published as *The Curious Bartender: An Odyssey of Malt, Bourbon & Rye Whiskies* in 2014. This abridged edition (with an expanded *Directory of Distilleries*) published in 2020 by
Ryland Peters & Small
20–21 Jockey's Fields
London WC1R 4BW
and
341 East 116th St
New York, NY 10029

www.rylandpeters.com

10 9 8 7 6 5 4 3 2

ISBN: 978-1-78879-213-4

A CIP record for this book is available from the British Library.

US Library of Congress CIP data has been applied for.

Printed in China

CONTENTS

FOREWORD

Whether you are curious about how a young whisky from Islay might taste, or interested in how history shaped whisky into the world's largest premium drinks category, or puzzled about how a barrel turns a fiery white spirit in to a mellow yet complex expression of time, or simply searching for better ways to enjoy drinking whisky – it's all here in this book. Because I was curious about these things I embarked upon an odyssey that helped me answer these questions and many more besides.

In 2015 my desire to learn more about whisky took me to some of the absolute extremities of the United Kingdom, through the 'bible-belt' states of Tennessee and Kentucky, on to the whisky bars of Taiwan and on bullet train rides along the length of Japan. I've rooted through the history books, looked into the origins of human civilisation, and visited state-of-the-art laboratories equipped with flavour detecting and creating technology concerned with whisky making. I have consumed whisky on remote wind-torn beaches as the sun rises, and in the world's tallest buildings as the sun sets. I've tasted £10,000 ($17,000) bottles and £10 ($17) bottles and found value in both of them. I've also made lifelong friends on this journey and spent a lot of time simply sitting, sipping and thinking about whisky all by myself...

This book is separated into three different sections. In the first, I have endeavoured to thoroughly explore the history of whisky, from the origins of alcoholic beverages and distillation and their seemingly inseparable connections to religion, philosophy and spirituality, through to the emergence of medicinal *aqua vitae*, *uisgebaugh* and 'whisky' itself. In more recent history, I explore some of the cultures, people and politics that have moulded whisky into the global product that we know today.

In part two, we take an in-depth look into whisky production, from a simple barley grain through to an amber liquid with unparalleled levels of complexity and intricacy. We also look at how some of the most traditional techniques, that still remain in practice today, are now balanced with impressive renewable energy standards and precise manipulation methods that craft distinct product over a period of years and decades.

The book includes some information on how best to drink and enjoy whisky, including some original cocktail recipes, innovative whisky serves and finally five unique whisky blend recipes, which can be constructed by anyone, and are made from whiskies that are readily available to everyone.

Finally, you will find a Glossary of whisky terminology and a Directory of Distilleries, encompassing whisky distilleries around the world – all active at the time of writing. Their particulars and peculiarities are summarized, as is what makes them unique in the world of whisky production.

PART ONE
THE HISTORY OF WHISKY

THE ORIGINS OF DISTILLATION

Distillation is an art based around scientific principles. Its history is a story of scientific technology and the cultural background of the various people who have attempted to master it. In the broadest sense it is a way of separating components of a liquid using heat, be it to purify or 'split' a liquid, or to extract the essence of a flower, leaf, fruit or plant in its potent vapours. It is this broad scope of distilling applications that has piqued mankind's curiosity for the past 5,000 years or so – whether it was a Chinese herbalist concentrating aromatic herbs into boozy steam, a Mesopotamian physician compounding roots and barks into a medicinal tincture, or a Greek philosopher defining the elements upon which the world is founded. The ins and outs of all of these antics will continue to be debated for the next 5,000 years no doubt, but the state of distillation today stands as a legacy to those crackpot experimenters who paved the way.

ANCIENT DISTILLING

It seems that most things of any great significance can be traced back to ancient Chinese civilization, and certainly the Chinese have a long history with alcohol. One excavation of a Neolithic settlement in China found a 9,000-year-old clay pot containing fermented rice remnants – presumably they didn't clean their pots very well, or perhaps the entire village dropped dead before anyone had a chance. Strange, though, that the first two literary references of Chinese distillation come from as late as the 12th century. It is possible that they were just late developers on this occasion, but both of the aforementioned references provide great detail of the ingredients, methods and various types of distillation, giving this reader the impression that by the 12th century these were very well-established practices indeed. Traditional Chinese literature is thin on the ground when it comes to technology and science

in general – the penning of classical literature has always been held in much higher regard in China – and adds further weight to the argument that they were more than familiar with alchemical arts at this time.

Some scholars believe that the Chinese knowledge of distillation was shared with Persian, Babylonian, Arabian and Egyptian merchants through their contact along the ancient silk-trading routes that trickled into the Middle East. These 2,000-mile trails were first carved out around the 10th century BC, but it took a good 700 years to really get established. Gold, jade, silk and spices were all up for grabs, but it was as a hub of cultural networking that the silk route really came into its own. It was, in effect, the information superhighway of its time.

Whether the Chinese got the know-how from the Indo-Iranian people, or the other way around, the secret knowledge of ardent waters and botanical vapours was beginning to condense down into the classical civilizations. And the pre-eminent philosophers, alchemists and botanists of these civilizations took great interest in it.

The Greek philosopher Aristotle was certainly aware of distillation in one shape or another. One section of his *Meteorologica* (circa 340 BC) concerns experiments that he undertook to distil

Aristotle

ABOVE The Great Library of Alexandria

liquids, discovering that 'wine and all fluids that evaporate and condense into a liquid state become water.'

In 28 BC a practising magus (magician) known as Anaxilaus of Thessaly was expelled from Rome for performing his magical arts, which included setting fire to what appeared to be water. The secrets of the trick were later translated into Greek and published around 200 AD by Hippolytus, presbyter of Rome. It turned out Anaxilaus had used distilled wine. Around the same time the Roman philosopher known as 'Pliny the Elder' (with a name like that he was surely endowed with a substantial beard) experimented with hanging fleeces above cauldrons of bubbling resin, and using the expansive surface area of the wool to catch the vapour and condense it into turpentine.

The world's first (self-proclaimed) alchemist, Zosimos of Panopolis, was also thought to be something of a wizard. He provided one of the first definitions of alchemy as the study of 'the composition of waters, movement, growth, embodying and disembodying, drawing the spirits from bodies and bonding the spirits within bodies.' It was Zosimos' belief that distillation in some way liberated the essence of a body or object that has led

to our definition of alcoholic beverages as 'spirits' today.

The scrolls and ledgers that documented all these works were largely preserved in the great libraries of the time. There is no better example of this than the ancient and epic Great Library of Alexandria, which was thought to have contained over 500,000 scrolls. That was until successive religious and political power struggles during the first half of the first millennium AD caused them to be either sold, stolen or, as was the case with Cleopatra and Julius Caesar, simply given away only to be burned. In the year 642, Alexandria was captured by a Muslim army and the last remaining remnants of the library were destroyed, and along with it the collective knowledge of much of the ancient world. Or so we thought... It would seem that some scraps of information and hastily copied texts still remained, written in ancient languages by long-dead men. The secrets to the mysteries of ardent waters and humid vapours did still exist, secreted away in monasteries and temples of learning dotted around Europe and the Middle East.

THE ORIGINS OF DISTILLATION

Islam

It was from these copied documents, amid the rise of the Islamic renaissance, that one fellow, Abu Musa Jabir ibn Hayyan (who in time became known simply as Geber), emerged in what stands as modern-day Iraq as the undisputed father of distillation. It is ironic that we have Islam, a religion that prohibits the drinking of alcohol, to thank for one of alcohol's most important breakthroughs. Some time around the end of the eighth century, Geber invented the first alembic still, which remains the basic form for all pot stills today. The major breakthrough in his still was that rather than using bits of sheep hair or an old rag to collect the spirit vapours, Geber's *al-ambiq* incorporated a condensing retort concocted by a pipe. With the alembic, Geber came tantalizingly close to understanding the full potential of distillation in what has to be one of the greatest understatements of all time: 'And fire which burns on the mouths of bottles due to boiled wine and salt, and similar

things with nice characteristics which are thought to be of little use, but are of great significance in these sciences.'

It is thought that Geber's discoveries were influenced by the works of Zosimos of Panopolis, and that it was not spirits he sought, but the philosopher's stone and the secret of turning base metals into gold. Geber was misguided in this particular instance, but his work on distillation inspired other Arab thinkers and tinkerers of the time to experiment with the art.

Possibly the earliest example we have of distilled spirits being consumed for enjoyment, rather than medicinally, comes from a poem written in Arabic by Abū Nuwās, who died in 814. In one poem he describes ordering three types of wine, each of which becomes stronger as the poem continues. For the final drink he asks for a wine that 'has the colour of rainwater but is as hot inside the ribs as a burning firebrand'.

But for the most part, through the ninth and 10th centuries, distilled spirit was used for medicinal purposes only. This was a time of great unsettlement in the world, however. Vikings raided and Crusades gathered momentum, and, as armies clashed and merchants traded, the seeds of understanding began to filter even into Dark Age Europe, where Latin-speaking scholarly monks had been waiting with eager patience for this wisdom of the ancients.

The knowledge remained exclusive to only the most worthy individuals, however. The 12th-century Italian chemist Michael Salernus wrote of 'liquid which will flame up when set on fire', but took measures to write his findings in code lest the information get into the wrong hands. Around 100 years later Arnaldus de Villa Nova, a professor from the University of Montpellier, successfully translated Arabic texts that revealed some secrets of distillation. He went on to write one of the first complete sets of instructions on

LEFT A 17th-century copper engraving of Arabian pioneer Abu Musa Jabir ibn Hayyan (Geber).

the distillation of wine, and it is this man that we have to thank for the term *aqua vitae* (water of life), a name which stuck in the Scandinavian *akvavit*, French *eaux de vie*, and of course the Scottish *uisge beatha*, which was later corrupted to whisky. Around 1300 he wrote: 'we call it aqua vitae, and this name is remarkably suitable, since it really is the water of immortality. It prolongs life, clears away ill humours, strengthens the heart, and maintains youth.'

FROM AQUA VITAE TO WHISKY

The big question that we need ask ourselves, though, is what were they doing with *aqua vitae*? The 14th and 15th centuries seem to be a transitional time for *aqua vitae* from its traditional use as a medical drug to a rather addictive social drug. Let us now focus on the British Isles, and chart the evolution of *aqua vitae* into the beverage known by the Gaelic name *uisge beatha* and its coming of age, as the world is introduced to whisky.

Irish legend cites that Saint Patrick brought distilling to Ireland in the fifth century. This seems like a bit of a stretch to me and a likely case of crediting the man simply because he is a prominent historical figure and, in fairness, a useful bloke to have around (especially where snakes were concerned). I have seen reference made to bronze distilling artefacts found around the ecclesiastical province of Cashel in Tipperary, but hard evidence of this is thin on the ground. What is a likely fact, however, is that Henry II discovered grain-distilling practices when he took the liberty of invading Ireland in 1172. If Henry got it right, it would indeed be one of the earliest examples of distilling in the British Isles that we know of.

There is some evidence to suggest that *aqua vitae* was being distilled in Ireland for non-medicinal use as far back as the 14th century. *The Red Book of Ossoly* (1317–1360), was a record of the diocese written by Richard Ledred, who was bishop, and it includes a treatise on *aqua vitae* made from wine, but makes no mention of grain-based spirits. In Edmund Campion's *History of Ireland*, which was published in 1571, he remarks that during the 1316 Irish Famine that was caused by a war with Scots soldiers, the miserable Irish comforted themselves 'with aqua vitae Lent long'. He also goes on to mention a Knight from shortly after the same time, who would serve to his soldiers 'a mighty draught of aqua vitae, wine, or old ale.'

This, of course, is not proof by itself of the consumption of *aqua vitae*, since Campion wrote the book 200 years after the event. Neither is the following eulogy, which is taken from a 1627 translation of *The Annals of Clonmacnoise*, originally published in 1408: 'Richard Magranell, Chieftain of Moyntyreolas, died at Christmas by taking a surfeit of aqua vitae, to him aqua mortis.'

Since the original 15th-century manuscript is lost, we can only guess at the accuracy of the translation and the poetic licence taken. The author's sense of humour in the pun '*aqua mortis*' (water of death) has not faded over the years, however, and surely there can be no greater testimony to the recreational enjoyment of *aqua vitae* at the start of the 15th century than the evidence of death through overindulgence during the festive period. Sadly, some things never change.

Raphael Holinshed describes the *aqua vitae* he finds in Ireland as a veritable cure-all for the 16th-century man, in his *Chronicles of England, Scotland and Ireland* (1577):

'Being moderatlie taken it sloweth age, it strengthneth youth, it helpeth digestion, it cureth flegme, it abandoneth melancholic, it relisheth the heart, it lighteneth the mind, it quickeneth the spirits, it cureth the hydropsie, it keepeth and preserveth the head from whirling, the eyes from dazeling, the tongue from lisping, the teeth from chattering, and the throte from ratling: the stomach from womblying, and the heart from swelling, the belly from retching, the guts from rumbling, the hands from shivering, & the sinews from shrinking, the veins from crumpling, the bones from aching, & the marrow from soaking.'

Taking the early Irish references at face value, it would seem that Scotland was a little slower on the uptake. The first reference to *aqua vitae* in Scotland comes from the Royal Exchequer Rolls of 1494 – which lists the sale of 500kg (1,120 lbs.) of malt to one Friar John Corr 'wherewith to make aqua vitae'. This order of *aqua vitae* was to be delivered to King James IV of Scotland no less. The story goes that King James had been campaigning on the island of Islay in the previous year and at some time or other got a taste for the spirit made there. A taste for it indeed, since the order placed in 1494 would be enough to manufacture over 1,200 bottles of whisky by today's standards!

Despite its apparent popularity with the royal household, it still took a while for *aqua vitae* to leave a mark on Scottish drinking habits. Most of the references to Scottish alcohol consumption during the following 50 years still refer to beer as the reliable beverage of the masses. *Aqua vitae* did, however, continue to exist for medical purposes. In 1505 a seal was granted by James IV of Scotland, which gave the Guild of Surgeon Barbers of Edinburgh (barbers were held in high regard back then) a monopoly over the manufacture of *aqua vitae*, stating that 'na [other] persons man nor woman within this Burgh make nor sell any aqua vitae within the samen'. And the Scots continued to find other uses for the stuff besides drinking it. In 1540 the treasurer's accounts contain an entry relating to the supply of *aqua vitae* for the manufacture of gunpowder.

Around the same time we saw Henry VIII, King of England, begin his long succession of failed relationships. When the Pope denied Henry a divorce from his first wife, Catherine of Aragon, Henry took matters into his own hands, and in 1534, made the unprecedented step of separating the Church of England from the Roman Catholic Church. Just to make sure the point was clear, he disbanded monasteries, priories, convents and friaries, leaving a lot of learned monks out in the cold. Some of these learned men integrated into the communities and the knowledge that had previously been the preserve only of these religious institutes began to filter through the land and into the farms and workshops of the very grateful common folk. Distilling gradually became a common farmyard practice, alongside brewing beer, churning butter and baking bread.

BELOW Henry VIII's dissolution of the monasteries drastically altered the landscape of England; one of its by-products was the dissemination of distillation knowledge among common folk, rather than just among monks.

During the same period it is likely that there were some significant advances in the equipment used to make drinkable spirits. Alcohol for medicinal purposes required very little in the way of still management, but if people were expected to drink and enjoy this peculiar tonic, the equipment would need to be slightly more tailored to the needs of safety and taste. Alembic stills became bigger, due to demand, which in turn improved the quality of the distillate through longer still necks. Conical-shaped stills, ranging up to some 44 gallons/53 US gallons in capacity became the industry – I use the term loosely – standard. 'Worm'-style condensers (see page 77) were also probably introduced, since they were known to be in use in France and Italy.

Fynes Moryson's *Itinerary of Ireland* (1603) gives us an early taste of the production method of 'good' Irish *aqua vitae* at this time, and provides us with one of the earliest examples of the corruption of the Gaelic name for 'water of life', *uisge beatha* (pronounced ooshky-bay):

'The Irish aqua vita, vulgarly called Usquebagh, is held in the best in the world of that kind, which is made also in England, but nothing so good as that which is brought out of Ireland. Usquebagh is preferred before our aqua vitas because the mingling of Raysons, Fennell seed and other things, mitigating the heat and making the taste pleasant, makes it lesse inflame and yet refresh the weake stomache with moderate heat and good relish.'

If you are thinking that this flavoured spirit sounds nothing at all like the whisky you enjoy today, you're not alone. It would seem that not everyone got the memo about whisky being made from only barley. In 1772 when Thomas Pennant visited the island of Islay he recorded that 'in old times the distillation was from thyme, mint, anise, and other fragrant herbs'. George Smith's *Compleat Body of Distilling* (1766) has a recipe and cost breakdown for 'Fine Usquebaugh' that has among its ingredients malt spirits, molasses spirits, mace, cloves, nuts, cinnamon, coriander, cubeb, raisins, dates, liquorice/licorice, saffron and sugar. This, to me, sounds remarkably like a (bad) gin, which is not at all surprising given the goings on of the gin craze that had been overwhelming London for the past half-century. Flavouring spirits was not only frequent during this time, but downright essential if one was inclined to make the concoction drinkable.

So there was no clear identity for *uisge beatha* during the 1600s, but that didn't hamper its steady integration into the fabric of society. More and more farms turned more of their attention to the profitable liquor and it developed into an important economic commodity, even being used as part of a rental payment for properties in Scotland and trading with Irish merchants – despite the apparent enthusiasm that the Irish held for making their own. And with the recognition of a growing industry, so too came the inevitable: taxes.

The first tax on spirits in Scotland was set in 1644 at a rate of 2 shillings and 8 pence for 'everie pynt of aquavytie or strong watteries sold within the countrey', with further increases half-a-dozen times over the following 60 years. After the Act of Union in 1707, the parliaments of England and Scotland were brought together as one, and the same taxes on distillation applied to both. In 1715, the English Malt Tax was put into effect in Scotland, too, and then increased in 1725, making it one of the major contributing factors to the Jacobite uprising and riots that were frequent at the time. But even with heavier taxes, the distilling industry continued to prosper, since *uisgebah* could also be made from other cereals. This fact also encouraged many of the brewers to turn to distilling.

Let's get one thing straight, though. For most of the 18th century, this still wasn't whisky as you know it. It was crudely distilled from a mixture of cereals in a rigged together tin can. The spirit wouldn't have been cut correctly, at best making it foul and at worst lethal; it was most likely flavoured, and certainly wouldn't have been intentionally rested in oak barrels. Besides, nearly all of the whisky produced during this time would have been for Scottish or Irish consumption, with London certainly needing no further encouragement to drink as its inhabitants wallowed in the midst of a gin craze.

There were exceptions to the backyard rule, of course. One of history's most prominent malt distilleries from the same period, and the first large distillery to flourish in Scotland, was Ferintosh. The distillery at Ferintosh became an incredibly lucrative operation after its owner was granted a tax break for support of the new Dutch king, William of Orange, who took to the British throne in 1689. No taxes meant the product could be sold cheaply, meaning the other tax-paying distilleries could not compete with Ferintosh.

Growth for Scottish distillers continued up until 1752, with the annual output almost doubling in the space of 10 years. The future looked good until disaster struck in 1757, marked by a massive crop failure that forced the British government to prohibit the sale of distilled spirits for three years. The use of a private still was not prohibited, however, and so long as its wares were sold only for household consumption, no law was broken. No enterprising Scotsman in his right mind would lie down just like that and so started illicit distilling and smuggling began on a massive scale. By the time the ban was lifted it was already too late – duty-free whisky had a good taste to it and men had little inclination towards paying taxes. And it was the game of taxation that seemed to govern the prevalence of illicit operations for the next 50 years, increasing dramatically when the risk of being caught was outweighed by the reward. A sudden increase in duty meant the sprouting up of new illicit distilleries by the thousands.

It seems the government was too slow to recognize that things were getting out of hand and excise officers were simply too lenient on those caught in the act of illicit distilling, with early records of some individuals being caught three or four times in a short period. When the authorities did get a handle on the sheer

ABOVE 17th- and 18th-century buildings, thought to be part of the old Ferintosh distillery in the Scottish Highlands.

scale of the problem, it was already endemic and far too big to police or manage, regardless of the severity of the punishment.

The risk to the clandestine operatives, of course, was not a particularly great one. The various inaccessible islands, glens and crags of the Highlands (many of which have given their names to present-day legitimate distilleries) provided ample seclusion from the prying eyes of the excise officers, who were also known as gaugers – named for their 'gauging' of the malt to assess its duty. The Glendronach Distillery in Speyside is one such operation that picked its location very carefully. Situated adjacent to natural springs, it meant that there was an abundance of clean water, but even better than that was the colony of rooks which nested nearby and were prone to screaming whenever anyone approached at night – as good a security alarm as anyone could wish for.

The 'legal' distilleries now had to compete on price with both the duty-free Ferintosh distillery, as well as illicit operations. Many of them reacted the only way that they could, and took measures to fake their customs and excise production declarations in an attempt to reduce their tax bill. The government got wise to this pretty quickly, though, and enforced a series of strict and oppressive measures that aimed to control the few remaining legitimate operations. In 1774 William Pitt's Wash Act was passed, which required Lowland stills to be a minimum of 400 litres/106 US gallons in capacity and taxed on their size, not their output. Highland distillers were granted more lenient taxes, based on the volume produced, and were permitted to use smaller stills of a minimum 91 litres/ 24 US gallons. The only problem was that they weren't allowed to sell it outside of the Highlands. The Wash Act drew a deep line in the sand between how Lowland and Highland distilleries operated, encouraging the distillers in the south to build stills that could distil very quickly, albeit with a significant drop in quality.

In the Highlands there was less rush, and the spirit was said to be of a much greater standard than the Lowland swill... but available only in the Highlands.

Distilling for personal consumption was outlawed in 1781. If the illegitimate distillers had ever thought about going back to the straight and narrow, those thoughts had completely gone out of the window by this point. As the 18th century drew to a close, the ongoing Highland Clearances, also known as the 'expulsion of the Gael', only served to fuel the fire of resentment that burned for the British government. Any perception in the Highlands that smugglers were wrongdoers or law breakers had been replaced by an acceptance of it as a profession and even as a god-given Gaelic right. Both the duty and the punishment for non-compliance were further increased, and Scots rebelled, resulting in what nearly amounted to all-out warfare.

The rate of taxation on whisky fluctuated greatly over the years, as much as tripling in war time when the British government needed the cash, and settling down again during times of peace.

Whisky would be distributed among towns and villages by 'bladdermen', so-called because concealed beneath their britches would be a bladder full of *uisge beatha*. Highland Park Distillery on the Orkney Islands was known to conceal casks of whisky in the hollow pillars of nearby St. Magnus Cathedral, despite the attending reverend reaffirming 'thou shalt not make whisky' in his Sunday service. During the same period it has been estimated that Edinburgh had around 400 distilleries; 11 of which were licensed.

The 1823 Excise Act changed everything, however. Duty on Scottish whisky was cut by more than 50%, down to the manageable rate of 2 shillings and 5 pence per gallon. For many business-minded distillers this was an opportunity to legitimize their operations and increase their business. The Glenlivet, Fettercairn, Cardhu, Balmenach and Ben Nevis are just some of the distilleries that are still operational today which saw their chance and licensed their operations during this time. By 1825 there were 263 licensed distilleries in Scotland, all of them free to produce whatever volume of spirit they wished. Quality naturally improved – since it is so much easier to make good whisky when you don't have to hide it from anyone – as did quantity, and the operations that chose to avoid the duty were soon forced out of the marketplace, with records of seizure in Scotland dropping from a post-Excise Act high of 764 in 1835 to only two in 1875.

However, the less documented illicit activity in Ireland was either on a considerably larger scale, or policed more vigorously (or both). In 1833 there were 8,233 reported cases of seizure of illicit distilling equipment and the numbers remained in the thousands even up until the 1870s.

The smuggling in Scotland didn't stop there, mind you, as tax on spirits was much higher in England than Scotland during the 19th century, by over 8 shillings a gallon. Licensed Scotch distillers, many of whom had plenty of experience of the smuggling lifestyle, developed ever more ingenious methods to smuggle their 'mountain dew' over the border, even going as far as to train dogs to swim across rivers with pig bladders full of whisky in tow. Practices like that were small time, however. There were bigger operations taking place as some estimates place the volume of Scottish duty-paid whisky crossing the border in the 1820s as upwards of 50,000 litres/10,000 US gallons every week (that's a lot of dogs). Many of the distillers would travel in armed groups, each carrying 30 litres/8 US gallons of spirit tied to themselves in metal canisters. Most of the time, excise officers were simply too scared to approach them – and who can blame them?

Even up until the 1980s it was normal for excise officers to live 'on site' at the distillery. One distillery manager once candidly told me that 'To be a distillery worker you have to have a real genuine love for drinking whisky, but to be an

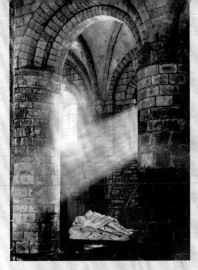

ABOVE The pillars of St. Magnus Cathedral on the Orkney Islands, some of which would have been secretly filled with casks of Highland Park whisky in the early years of the 19th century, unbeknownst to the vicar!

excise officer you have to have an even bigger love.'

Back in the 1970s at The Bowmore Distillery on Islay, twin brothers John and Roger McDougall were the acting customs excise officers – just to make things even more confusing. The brothers apparently had a passion for making their own spirits, Alastair McDonald from Auchentoshan tells me. While working at The Bowmore at the tender age of 17, he was cornered by the two big officers and asked: 'What do you drink, McDonald?' Alastair assumed that something had gone missing in the distillery and quickly replied, 'Nothing.' The brothers produced a bottle of something dark and held it under his nose, apparently looking for a response. When none was given they told young Alastair to drink the liquid, which tasted like coffee. Alastair gave the pair a pleading look, and they responded by telling him 'It's our homemade Tia Maria – d'ya like it?'

The story of distillation in North America starts with rum. The early colonists didn't trust water, so turned to hard cider and beer as their staple beverages. However, something stronger was needed for the cold winter nights, and rum was the answer. Rum flooded into North America from the Caribbean during the 1600s, as well as sugar and molasses – the building blocks required to make one's own rum. Many households owned rickety alembic stills that could be used to distil mead, pear cider and hard cider into spirit – a job invariably conducted by the woman of the house – but the cheap and ready supply of molasses made rum the most economic choice for those seeking intoxication. In 1750 Peter Kalm, a Swedish-Finnish traveller, noted in his *Travels into North America* that colonists believed rum to be a healthier choice over imported spirits made from grain, even going as far as to point out that fresh meat stored in rum will 'keep as it was' while in other spirits it would be 'eaten full of holes.'

Nevertheless, there are records of corn and rye beers being made in Connecticut from the middle of the 17th century. In fact, the earliest known record of any kind of distillation in North America is of the Dutch on Staten Island (which was a Dutch Colony at the time) in 1640. The distiller was William Kieft, and he also owned a tavern, which was the only place you could buy his creations. Bottled products included brandy and some kind of crude whiskey made from the leftover dregs of beer. This was a relatively common practice in the years to come, since grain was much more expensive than molasses.

Jump forward 100 years, and not much on the back bar has changed, but rye and corn-based spirits were beginning to gain popularity. George Washington, a man who clearly liked a drink, operated one of the largest distilleries in North America out of his Mount Vernon Estate in Virginia; it was making rye whiskey. During the American War of Independence he was known to remark that 'The benefits arising from the moderate use of strong liquor have been experienced in all armies and are not to be disputed.' The same man had a barrel of Barbados rum delivered to celebrate his inauguration as the first President of the United States in 1789.

Corn whiskey probably lagged behind rye a bit. Maize was still an exotic, New World commodity, whilst the rye that had been brought over by German settlers originally was a familiar Old World product that was easy to cultivate and familiar to brewers and distillers. As settlers expanded the frontiers and headed south, into modern day Kentucky and Tennessee, the soil and climate changed. Where rye flourished in the colder north, colonists soon learned from native Americans that 'Indian Corn' crops grew better in the humid heat. Not only that, but corn could even be planted in-between other crops and even trees without the need for levelling off the land beforehand. Just like the gold rush of the mid-1800s, the difference being that this gold was edible, New-Worlders flocked to the area to stake their claim on land and to grow this energy-packed, new-fangled

ABOVE George Washington's Mount Vernon mansion in Virginia in the late 18th century. In 1797, he hired a Scottish plantation manager, who encouraged him to build a whiskey distillery. By 1799, the distillery they had created was the largest in the United States.

food source. Some of these early settlers had familiar names like Beam and Weller. They, along with many others, were the forefathers of the great whiskey tycoons of the 19th century.

Corn was exported by the boat- and barrel-load. The two major trading routes from the western frontier went either to the Eastern seaboard, or down-river to New Orleans. Without railroads or motor vehicles, both were long, arduous journeys that required a significant animal and human workforce to cart the barrels of milled corn. It made far more sense to convert the corn into liquor and pop that in the barrel instead. With the weight reduced by 80%, but the value remaining the same, a horse gained its independence five times the load. Distillation operations popped up like worms out of the ground: basic as can be and dangerous to boot. These were not artisans crafting fine-quality liquor; they were always ancillary to farm·operations, made by business-minded farmers, reducing costs and maximizing profit.

The production network was established. What was needed next was a market for the product. Politics was the answer – America gained its independence in 1789. The 'Demon Rum' that had built the colonies was a British invention and a recent memory of colonial rule that had birthed the slogan 'No taxation without representation'. President John Adams himself admitted that 'Molasses was an essential ingredient in American Independence.' Rum was most definitely out of favour. The United States looked inwards for a new spirit of America. The answer was whiskey.

It is a historical fact that when there is big demand for a product, as there was

with whiskey during this time, there will always be a taxman ready· to take his cut. Continuing to mirror the goings on in Scotland 150 years previously, in 1791, only two years after independence, an excise duty on spirits was passed that required cash payment to the government based on the production of spirits. The aim was to make up the huge deficit that the war had cost the nation, but farmer-distillers felt cheated – the independence that many of them had fought for during the war was being pulled out from underneath them. It sparked rebellion, which was particularly prevalent on the southwestern frontier and across the Appalachian region that stretched all the way from New York down to South Carolina. The new government demonstrated for the first time that it was willing to use violence to suppress the uprising, but collection of taxes was minimal and the tax was repealed in 1802. Sixty years later it was reinstated, but it was much less of a problem at that time, since the government was buying huge stocks of whiskey to fire up its Civil War troops.

BOURBON

It's fairly easy to work out where rye, corn, Canadian *et al.* got their names, but to Brits, bourbon is a type of chocolate biscuit/cookie, right? To tell that tale we must first look to France. Louis XVI was King of France from 1774 to 1792, and a strong ally of George Washington during the War of Independence. As a sign of America's gratitude to Louis – mostly for supplying weapons – after the war, a huge swathe of land that included 34 modern-day Kentucky counties was named after Louis' house name, Bourbon. Some say that it was actually the French general and war hero Lafayette, also descended from the French royal house, who the county was named after. Either way, the Americans liked the French during this period – Bourbon County was an obvious reflection of that.

As time went on, the French connection was forgotten and Bourbon County got smaller. The state of Kentucky was formed, but 'Old Bourbon County' whiskey continued to be traded in New Orleans. As the barrels of liquor bobbed up and down the Mississippi River (not literally – they would of course have been on a boat) towards the port, they had lots of time to mellow and integrate with the wood in the southern sun. The whiskey became famous for its quality and the name of bourbon became synonymous with it.

The title of being the first producer of bourbon is a hotly contested one. Many attribute it to Evan Williams in 1783, though solid evidence to back it up is scarce. Others pick out the preacher, Elijah Craig, claiming that he was the first to age whiskey in barrels. Allegedly, Craig used barrels that previously held pickled fish (for reasons of economics, not flavour); so as to remove the smell, he would char the inside. The simple act of charring a barrel opened up a whole new world of whiskey complexity to his liquid.

Other historians believe that the char was a sterilizing measure, put in place during a time when casks were used for fermentation of the wash. Then there are Oscar Pepper and James Crow, distillers through the 1830s and 1840s who perfected many of the methods that are essential to good bourbon production today. Bourbon whiskey is not a product of any single man's endeavours, but a concerted effort by many men, across multiple generations, compelled and coerced for reasons of economics, geography and the pursuit of a better product and a stronger brand. And what we do know is that the first known advertisement for bourbon whiskey was published in the *Western Citizen* newspaper, in Paris, Kentucky in 1821.

The mid-1800s saw the introduction of the column that still exists in many a bourbon whiskey distillery. This meant an increase in production, due to the continuous nature of the apparatus. It also meant greater consistency – another strong selling point to the thirsty public. As frontiers stretched out to the Old West, it was bourbon whiskey that cowboys called for in saloons.

In 1850, the Louisville & Nashville Railroad was chartered and began connecting Louisville to markets not serviced by the traditional steamboat trade. The growing railway system caused a significant change in the bourbon industry. Distilleries no longer had to be located near gristmills or flowing streams or rivers. The railroad could bring large quantities of grain to nearly any location in the state and could transport full barrels of whiskey to market. This allowed bourbon distilleries to locate in Louisville and offer a better service to the whiskey merchants on 'Whiskey Row'. For example, the Old Kentucky Distillery was established in 1855 along a railway on the outskirts of Louisville. And in 1860, the Early Times Distillery was built at the Early Times Rail Station in nearby Nelson County – it is still there today.

When the Civil War broke out in 1861, Kentucky, a border state, found itself

ABOVE Bourbon County in Kentucky is named in honour of Louis XVI's family name, in thanks for supplying weapons to George Washington during the War of Independence.

ABOVE Louisville, the largest city in Kentucky, in 1872.

trapped between both sides of the conflict. The fact that Kentucky remained part of the Union, but still permitted the ownership of slaves, made it about as neutral as was possible. Some stories from that time suggest that when Union soldiers were in town it would be the American flag that was flown, and when Confederates came by it would be the Confederate flag. Both armies drank bourbon recreationally, as well as using it for cleaning wounds and no doubt raising spirits.

The end of the Civil War also saw the introduction of a government-controlled distillery licensing system. This system made small-scale distilling a legally cumbersome and expensive activity. The days of small-batch production and the farmer-distiller tradition were numbered.

In Louisville, the bourbon business saw the development of new trading houses, including J. T. S. Brown (later Brown-Forman). These companies resumed the practice of buying whiskey in bulk from rural and city-based distillers and vatting them together to create proprietary flavour profiles. The vatted whiskies were then rebarreled for sale in bulk lots to wholesalers, retailers, doctors and pharmacists.

As a new century closed in, everything was looking good for American whiskey. In fact, it would have been perfect were it not for the murmurs of temperance coming from the sidelines. Those murmurs were gradually turning into shouts, and it slowly became clear that Prohibition wasn't far away. And with it would come the near-complete collapse of the entire whiskey industry. Things would never be the same again.

CANADA

In Canada, the earliest known occurrence of distilling goes back to James Grant's rum distillery in Quebec City, around 1767. As is usual, it is the cheapest ingredient that gets distilled first, and during that period the cheapest ingredient was molasses. But one thing Canada was not short of was land, and the colonists soon got to work planting all manner of crops.

In terms of brewing and distilling, it was probably Scottish immigrants who kicked things off, which might be why Canadians, like the Scots, drop the 'e' from their spelling of whisky. Either way, Canada was a melting pot of experienced booze producers from France, Scotland, Ireland and England. Each European nation had brought its own cereal offering to the table, too. The Dutch and Germans came with rye; the English brought barley and wheat. Indigenous corn flourished in the south and rye did just as well in the cooler northern areas.

But the most popular cereal for distilling in the early 1800s was wheat. Wheat was milled down for bread-making, and the glamorous-sounding but apparently not particularly useful 'wheat middlings' were sent to be mashed and distilled. Barley was malted and used for its enzymatic benefits, and eventually rye became a seasoning of pepper over the top of the 'mash bill': the different grains used for mashing.

One of the first whisky distilleries, and certainly the most successful of its era, was that of the Molson family of Montreal. Molson is the second-oldest company in all of Canada and better known for its brewing empire. But before beer became their bread and butter, Thomas, the son of founder John Molson, took a trip to Scotland in 1816 and embarked on a tour around a bunch of distilleries. He recorded what he saw, and, convinced that whisky was the next big thing in Canada, built his own distillery a few years later. Other whisky distilleries materialized, keen to get a piece of the pie, and in 1827, only six years after Molson had sold his first bottle, there were 31 known distilleries in lower Canada. Another six years later and that number is believed to have tripled in size.

Reports from this time indicate that this 'whisky' may have been distilled only once, meaning that it was likely no more than 20% ABV and more than a little 'ragged' around the edges. Exported stuff, by Molson at least, was apparently distilled twice in order to ensure its survival on the long voyage over to the United Kingdom or across the United States.

In 1840, distilling licences were up for grabs and reports from the time show that there were over 200 distilleries across Canada; today there are fewer than a dozen. The demand for Canadian rye whisky was high as well. In 1861, America was thrown into Civil War, where whiskey distilling was outlawed in the South (stills were used to make cannons) and heavily taxed in the North. Canadian whisky happily picked up the slack and the void was filled. In 1887 Canada was the first nation to put a minimum ageing requirement on whisky. The minimum age was one year, which was increased to two years in 1890.

Canada played an important role during Prohibition in the USA, providing a steady flow of liquor, namely Canadian Club – which has had a strong following ever since, to thirsty American people. At the height of Prohibition there were thought to be over 1,000 bottles of Canadian Club crossing the US border every day.

These days, Canadian whiskies share similar mash bills to that of bourbon – corn-dominated, but with some rye or wheat overtones. There are some 100% rye whiskies, too, most notably those produced by Alberta Distillers Ltd.

Up until this stage in our story, whisky made in Scotland was sold and produced only as a single product from a single distillery. The Excise Act of 1823 encouraged illicit distillers to hit the straight and narrow, and many did, but even after that you would have been hard-pushed to find a bottle of Scotch whisky outside of Scotland, and over 90% of the malt whisky made in Scotland never crossed the border. Winston Churchill once attested to this: 'My father would never have drunk whisky, except when shooting on a moor or in some very dull, chilly place. He lived in an age of brandy and soda.' The truth is that the whisky of the early 19th century could not compete with the finesse of French brandies. The changeover kicked off in 1830, but it would take another 60 years for all of the cogs to align correctly and for Scotch to make its true impact on the world.

THE DEVELOPMENT OF THE CONTINUOUS STILL

It started with new advances in distillation. Whisky had always been made the same way, fermented from malted barley and distilled in a big onion-shaped kettle. It was a time-consuming 'batch' process that produced only a little liquor for a lot of effort, and required the cleaning and resetting of all the equipment before it could be repeated. At the time it was also highly inconsistent, almost all of the 330 or so distilleries had previously run as illicit smuggling operations, and despite their now legitimate operations, many of their practices remained crude, inconsistent and 'boutique', to put it nicely. But this was the early 1800s and with the industrial revolution grinding into motion, an

alternative was needed to the primitive ways of old: a device that could continuously distil alcohol.

Irishman Aeneas Coffey is usually credited with inventing the first continuous still in 1830. However, those of us in the know are aware that the true inventor was actually Robert Stein, in 1827. But what most people don't know is that Stein actually relied on earlier designs to make his still, too. To discover more about that we must travel to 19th-century France.

Despite being illiterate, French-born Édouard Adam attended chemistry lectures under Professor Laurent Solimani at the University of Montpellier. Adam developed and patented the first type of column still in 1804, except the column was horizontal rather than vertical and based on laboratory Woulfe bottles (sequential bottles linked by pipes). It worked by linking together a series of what Adam called 'large eggs', with pipes that would transfer alcohol vapour from one to the next. The concentration of alcohol increased in each subsequent egg, while the leftover stuff was recycled back at the start. It wasn't truly continuous in its design, but it certainly paved the way for stuff that came later down the line.

Adam died in 1807, but his rivals continued to improve the design, with such inventions as the Pistorius still, patented in 1817, which was the first still to be in a column shape. Steam was pumped up from the bottom and beer from the top and distillation took place

RIGHT Frenchman Édouard Adam built upon the principle of the Woulfe bottle and in 1801 patented the first still to produce alcohol in one operation.

on a series of plates. The feints were recycled and fed in again at the top.

Subsequent iterations were developed by the French engineer Jean-Baptiste Cellier Blumenthal and a mysterious Englishman known only as Mr Dihi. It tended to be the case that these stills incorporated one or two elements of the continuous still as we now know it, but never all of them working in unison. It wasn't until Robert Stein came along that it eventually happened.

Robert Stein came from strong distilling stock. His father, James Stein, established the Kilbagie Distillery in Fife in 1777, one of the largest distilleries of its era. Robert went on to run it, and with the new Excise Act in place, he set about expanding his legal operation. Stein patented a new type of still, shaped like a column and split into a series of small chambers. The wash was pre-heated, then pumped into the chambers where it came into contact with steam. As the vapour rose, the steam stripped the spirit away, and anything that wasn't alcohol condensed on one of the fine hair meshes that were dotted around inside the contraption. Spirit and waste were collected separately and the process continued.

The patent still was a licence to print alcohol, but on the negative side, the purchase of a patent still was a huge investment, costing many times more than a simple pot still. But this type of distillation produced a much lighter, cleaner and more delicate spirit that was cheaper to produce and up to 94% ABV. (For a more detailed look at the continuous still, see page 80.)

Just as the first orders of Stein's still were being delivered, another still was invented. An Irishman named Aeneas Coffey, who had formerly been the Inspector General of Excise in Dublin (and had no doubt seen a few stills in his time), patented his still in 1830. It had a few marked improvements over Stein's: larger processing power (3,000 gallons/3,600 US gallons of wash in an hour), greater purity of distillate (up to 96% ABV) and a much cleaner design. One of the best parts of the new 'patent still' was that pipes containing the cool wash entering the system doubled up as condensing coils for the hot alcohol vapours exiting it – like a dog eating its own tail. It was a work of genius for its time, reflected in the fact that it is still the same basic design that is used all over the world today.

The first continuous stills were made from iron, and the results were apparently disgusting – so bad, in fact, that the spirit was passed on to gin distillers to be re-distilled and flavoured. Experiments then took place with copper and wooden continuous stills, and the favourite today is, of course, steel.

Stein's design quickly lost favour, the last one being installed at Glenochil in 1846. Coffey's went on to dominate and became a favourite of the Lowland distillers, marking a clear divergence of Lowland distillers from the Highland style, which still remains in place today. This divergence from one another would later become a huge matter of dispute between the traditional malt distillers of the North, and the industrial grain distillers of the South. They were producing two entirely different products – the powerfully flavoured malt whisky was in shorter supply, inconsistent and costly, while there was an abundance of the bland grain whisky, so much so, that the distillers were finding it hard to shift it all. The solution was blending.

BLENDS

Blends, both then and now, comprised a mixture of malt and grain whiskies. The malts were mixed together to give a uniform and balanced flavour, while the grain acted as the lighter backdrop. The invention of blending was of mutual benefit to both parties, as it combined the gentle characteristics of the grain with the powerful flavours of the malt in a uniform and pliable mixture.

There is some evidence to suggest that blending was going on right at the start of the 1800s. During that time many of

ABOVE/RIGHT Advertisements for well-known whisky blenders of the 19th and 20th centuries.

the most famous names in blended whisky were working in grocers' stores or as tea blenders or wine merchants. Blending back then would have been conducted on a very personal level, however, with 'A bit of this and a bit of that for you, Mr. Douglas', etc. And it wasn't until much later, in 1860, that this changed.

The Spirits Act of 1860 allowed whisky to be blended under bond, before the duty had been paid on it, meaning that blending could be done on a much larger scale. This was one of the main catalysts for the rise of the blends. The promise of blended whisky provided new avenues of trade, with larger mass appeal, larger production potential and lower costs. Also, because blends were more consistent, consumers could pick a favourite and know that it could be relied upon, meaning that a greater emphasis could be placed on the brand and marketing of the product.

The legislation coincided very well with the construction of Scotland's rail network and its connection with northern English cities. Rail networks were also

established between Edinburgh and Glasgow, but also rail lines connecting Inverness, Aberdeen and Keith (right in the heart of Speyside) were launched in the 1850s. Suddenly it had become a lot easier to move whisky around the place.

The final piece of good fortune that set Scotch on its way was the decimation of the French wine and brandy industry by the phylloxera vine louse, an event that all but killed off brandy and set the industry back 20 years. With highly limited stocks of brandy, people turned to the next brown spirit on the list: whisky.

In my opinion it is the combination of the two factors, brandy's collapse and what was effectively the invention of blending, that had the greatest hand in putting whisky where it is today.

Blending was also the driving force behind improving the image of Scotch whisky at a time where marketing was just as important as product quality. This drove demand for grain whisky as well as for malt, as both were needed to make blends, and in the latter part of the 19th century the whisky industry in Scotland had a clear split. For every litre/quart of pot still malt whisky that was made, two litres/quarts of patent still grain were produced. In 1877 the six major producers of grain whisky amalgamated their operations under the title of Distillers Company Limited (DCL). They effectively became self-regulating, manufacturing all of the grain whisky for the blends.

The gold rush had begun and dozens of malt distilleries opened in Scotland during the 1890s, keen to meet the blenders' needs. Roughly one-fifth of the malt distilleries that are operational in Scotland today were opened between 1893 and 1899.

Many were doomed to fail, though, as in the following years the market became saturated with malt whisky stocks eager to find their way into the blender's bottle. Despite seemingly good prospects, the bandwagon was well and truly loaded, everyone had overestimated the demand for whisky, and well-established firms like Edinburgh-based blender, J & G Stewart, went into liquidation in 1898, taking down dozens of others with it through the network of credit. The entire industry was threatened with collapse as a result, and vast stocks of whisky remained stationary in warehouses. This event and others around it marked the beginning of 50 years of zero growth for whisky in Scotland.

THE BARONS OF BLENDING

In the space of 20 years, a select group of Scots, later known as the 'whisky barons', built an unprecedented global market off of the growing popularity for blended whisky. Their good timing, coupled with a shrewd sense of self-marketing, afforded them not just worldwide domination of the drinks market, but lofty positions within high society and the eyes and ears

of politicians and royalty alike. The names Buchanan, Mackie, Usher, Walker and Dewar can be seen behind the counter of off-licence and liquor stores around the world today, but only because the men behind them forged an industry for blended whisky when the world needed it most.

In 1885, Tommy Dewar, the fifth son of John Dewar of Perth, arrived in London at the tender age of 21. His mission was to make the Dewar's brand of whisky that his father had established in 1846 a household name. Allegedly Tommy had only two business contacts in London when he arrived – one of whom turned out to be bankrupt, and the other dead. Unfazed, Tommy set about establishing himself as the premier Scotsman in London. It seems to me that Tommy's subsequent success was based upon a solid foundation of charm, wit and intelligence. It worked, though – between 1894 and 1897 Dewar's quadrupled its capital. Tommy himself was made Sheriff of London in 1896, the same year that Dewar's began building the Aberfeldy malt distillery in his home town. During that same period Tommy can also lay claim to owning the third motor vehicle ever sold in England – if such a thing as celebrities existed at the time, 'Whisky Tom' was certainly one of them. Dewar's was also the first whisky brand to use paper labels, back in 1863.

Then there was James Buchanan, another formidable character from the age of blending – with a streak of red hair, tall and wiry, and famous for his mantra 'A man must make his opportunity, as oft as find it'. If Tom Dewar was the larger-than-life Scotsman about town, Buchanan was the lean, graceful figure, demanding the attention

ABOVE The Scottish whisky distiller Tommy Dewar, who along with his brother John, built their family label, Dewar's, into a successful international brand.

of everyone present while he quietly smouldered in the corner of the room. After moving to London in 1879, his famous Black & White blend, originally known as 'Buchanan's Blend' but affectionately re-dubbed due to its white label on a black bottle packaging, became the official whisky of the House of Commons only a year after JB established his business in London. In 1903, Buchanan & Co went public, but all £850,000 worth of shares were purchased by the man himself – he was truly a one-man mega-corporation. A few years later, Buchanan was knighted for his services to the country and then, in 1922, awarded a peerage and the title of Lord Woolavington, a name that he apparently made up when once signing a cheque to a politician in whom he placed little trust.

From the town of Kilmarnock in East Ayrshire hailed the Walker family. Kilmarnock was an up-and-coming place in the early 19th century, famous in particular for its threaded rugs and carpets. The first Scottish railway was laid in the town in 1812 and it was on Kilmarnock's King Street that John Walker opened his grocer's store in 1820 at the tender age of 15. One of the services Walker was famed for was his tea blending – he later applied the same methods to blending whisky. John's son, Alexander, joined the business around the same time that the blending laws were slackened. Alexander was every bit as visionary as Dewar and Buchanan, even in the early days of the humble Kilmarnock grocers. Alexander looked outwards and to the potential of Walker's Kilmarnock Whisky in the American and global markets. Alexander Walker was the true driving force behind his father's brand and the inspiration for his son, Alexander II, who took the reins when Alexander died in 1889. By that point the Walker brand was unstoppable. In 1893 the company bought out the entire Cardhu Distillery in Speyside, a whisky that became a key piece to its Old Highland Blend, which later became known simply as Black Label. Over the 25 years that

BUCHANAN'S

"BLACK & WHITE"
LEADS
JAMES BUCHANAN & Cº Lᵀᴰ GLASGOW & LONDON
SCOTCH WHISKY DISTILLERS

ABOVE Buchanan's Black & White whisky achieved notoriety in literature, as it was ordered both by James Bond in *Moonraker* and Dick Driver in F. Scott Fitzgerald's *Tender is the Night*.

followed, Johnnie Walker became the biggest blended whisky in the world, and a globally recognized brand name before Coca-Cola had even left Atlanta. In 1908, over a lunchtime meeting, the pre-eminent black-and-white artist of the day, Tom Brown, sketched the image of the 'striding man' on a napkin – it remains one of the most internationally recognized logos in the world today.

Dewar, Buchanan and Walker were not the only hard-working men who possessed the vision and determination to see their businesses prosper. Others equally worthy of a mention are the Haigs, Mackies and Berry Brothers. In 1824, the Haigs were also the founders of the Cameronbridge Distillery in Fife, which is today responsible for making a large proportion of Diageo's entire grain whisky, vodka and gin portfolio. Its Gold Label and Dimple brands became popular

JOHN WALKER, ESQ.
OF KILMARNOCK. SCOTLAND,
on his pedestrian hobby-horse.

"IT TAKES ME A LONG TIME TO GET ROUND"
said Johnnie Walker

"The road to Kilmarnock," said Johnnie Walker, "is a long one; in fact it takes me years to get there. For the separate whiskies, which are blended at Kilmarnock into Johnnie Walker, have first of all to mature for years in the wood. Only by ageing naturally in oak casks can these fine whiskies develop the qualities which enable them to be blended into a harmonious, 'round' whisky—so that's why it takes me so long to get 'round.'

"You will understand now why maturing and blending play such an important part in the special enjoyment you get from Johnnie Walker—and, understanding, *ask for Johnnie Walker by name*."

JOHNNIE WALKER
Born 1820—still going strong

products, and in 1906 it was appointed the official purveyor of whisky to the House of Lords.

Glasgow-based James Mackie created his White Horse brand, unique in its use of Lagavulin in the blend. He was also at the centre of the debate around 'What is whisky?' that kicked off in 1905. At the time, Highland distillers were up in arms over the 'lesser' grain spirit that was beginning to dominate the category and a big legal battle ensued, ultimately finding that, despite being different, the patent-still spirits had every right to be classed as Scotch. Mackie, who had interests in both sides of the debate, involved himself heavily in the argument but took a neutral standpoint, arguing that, regardless of the name, Scotch whisky should always be well aged and of good quality. It was Mackie's input that ultimately led to the regulations requiring Scotch whisky to be aged for a minimum of three years.

London-based wine merchant Berry Brothers & Rudd knew a good opportunity when it saw it. The Volstead Act had taken effect in America, meaning the production, sale, import and export of alcohol over 0.5% ABV was illegal. That of course didn't stop some people, and the demand for spirits was high. In 1921, Francis Berry was introduced to one Captain William McCoy in a hotel bar in Nassau, Bahamas. The Bahamas acted as the go-between for new bootleg spirits being shipped over to American soil – a kind of middleman to ease the conscience of the importer. McCoy was the courier, one of the best there was, granting his quality products the catchphrase 'the real McCoy'. Cutty Sark became a sign of good-quality whisky on the East Coast of the US during a time where moonshiners and backroom distillers were bottling up chemical cocktails and flogging them as potable spirits.

DEFINING WHISKY

The events taking place at the time perpetuated the feeling of unease among the malt distillers, as their numerous but comparatively small operations were already at the beck and call of the huge Distillers Company and multinational blending houses. All but a few malt producers were completely reliant on selling all of their products to blenders for bottling, marketing and selling. The blenders held so much power, in fact, that they could drive down prices of malt whisky through fear that the distillery owner would no longer be able to shift his wares. But if the blending houses failed, so did the malt distilleries.

Malt whisky producers began petitioning for a firm legal definition of what whisky actually is, while grain whisky distillers advertised with slogans like 'not a headache in a gallon' as a means of baiting their pot-still cousins. What followed later became known as the 'What is whisky?' debate, led by the appointment of a royal commission on 'whisky and other potable spirits'. The malt distillers of the Highlands argued that only 100% malt whisky made in the traditional manner (pot still) should be classified as the true whisky of Scotland. Grain-whisky makers, along with blenders – who, through their prolific use of grain whisky in their blends, also had a lot at stake – argued that their product was of

equal, if not greater worth, and had every right to be listed as Scotch whisky. The malt whisky producers relented slightly and admitted that any blend containing at least 50% malt whisky was alright with them, but even then they were outnumbered and outgunned. For starters, many of the Highland malt whisky distilleries had already been bought out by DCL, meaning that their forces were not at all united. Then there was the fact that their product was generally viewed as being a little rough around the edges when consumed by itself. Couple that with the fact that blended whisky accounted for almost all of the bottle sales of whisky made in Scotland and it doesn't take a genius to work out where the chips would fall.

The 1909 report effectively lumped malt, grain and blended 'whiskey' into the same category, with no minimum requirements for blending and not even a minimum age statement at this stage. It was a huge win for the grain whisky makers.

At the turn of the 20th century, the biggest whisky blenders in Scotland were Walker's, Dewar's and Buchanan's. By 1909, whisky was the most widely consumed spirit in Britain and the biggest export markets were Australia, Canada, South Africa and the United States. But despite all that, the industry had still been over-optimistic about growth and no one was running at their full production potential. Things were about to get even worse, though...

Before we go into that, here are a couple of important points on etymology. For the first time in 1715 we finally see our favourite drink referred to in a manner that seems more familiar. Below is a snippet of a verse from a military poem, which is entitled 'A Dialogue between his Grace the Duke of Argyle, and the Earl of Mar':

Perhaps we may Recruit again,
And that we'll let you ken, Sir;
If that once more we shall engage,
We shall know how it goes, Sir,
Whiskie shall put our brains in rage,

And snuff shall prime our nose, Sir,
With swords and guns into our hands
We'll stoutly venture on, Sir

The earliest reference to the word 'whisky' (with a 'y') that I could find pre-dates any that I have before seen in print or on the Internet. It comes from the letter book of Bailie John Steuart. On 13th September 1735 he writes concerning a consignment of herring designated for Loch Broom. Also on the shipment are:

[...] 21 pounds Candles, a half stone butter, four pecks peese, thirty six pound Roll Tobacco, and five Gallon whisky;

And since we started in Ireland, we had better end there, too. By far my favourite early use of 'whisky', and yet another that I have not before seen in print, comes from a poem entitled 'The Honest Irishman's Wish', first printed in *The London Magazine and Monthly Chronologer* in 1738:

The folly of pride; for we're always allow'd
To be, first proud of nothing; then,
    proud of being proud.
Of Brandy, or wine, I could wish to
    have none,
Whether genuine or brew'd, from the
    Loyre (Loire) or Garrone.
Were we but as wise as we're poor,
    I should think
Good beer, ale, and whisky, might serve
    us for drink.

THE NAMING OF WHISKY

As we already know, 'whiskey' with an 'e' is the current spelling used for Irish and American spirits and without the 'e' for Scottish, Canadian and Japanese 'whisky'. It hasn't always been this way, however, and it would seem that our forefathers were a lot less pedantic about keeping the origins segregated in the past. There are plenty of examples in the early 20th

century of Irish whiskey being spelled with no 'e', and the Royal Commission of 1908 that offered the first legal definition of Scotch spelled it with an 'e'. Indeed, American whiskey, although usually spelled with an 'e' (there are a few brands such as Maker's Mark, George Dickel and Early Times that spell their product 'whisky') is by legal definition, even today, spelled with no 'e'.

So what's this all about? Well, the story goes that many Irish and American producers (particularly those of Irish descent) dropped the 'e' from their whisky in the 1870s as a means of disassociating themselves with the inferior Scottish product. Whether this is true or not, it would appear that it has stuck now, the irony being that many people consider Scotch whisky to be the prized jewel among whiskies today.

THE DARK AGES

The following 20 years were a nightmare for the industry as World War I set in, and taxes were increased by the Liberal Chancellor Lloyd George in what he called the 'People's Budget' – which introduced pensions, national insurance and unemployment benefit. George was a family man and a teetotaller himself, and perhaps whisky's greatest adversary at the time. During World War I, he commented that 'Drink is doing more damage than all the German submarines put together' and proposed that the taxes on spirits (not wine and beer) should be doubled.

Many malt distilleries cut their losses and merged to protect their interests. Blenders did, too, most notably Buchanan's and Dewar's, which were later joined by Walker's and DCL.

Across the pond things were even worse. Many bourbon distilleries were forced to manufacture gunpowder in place of whiskey. What came next, though, all but killed the entire industry.

Prohibition came into effect on 17th January 1920 and lasted a full 13 years. The sale, consumption, importation and manufacture of alcohol in the USA became illegal and almost all of the American whiskey distilleries were forced to close, never to re-open. There were a few exceptions, however, and some distilleries were kept afloat by applying for a medical licence, since even then, whiskey was considered to be of use to the medical industry. Brown-Forman was among them, but it bought the Early Time distillery to help bolster its stocks.

Scotch whisky had only achieved limited success up until that point anyway, while bourbon remained the American staple. The same rules that applied to bourbon applied to Scotch, however, so blenders clambered to make their product available medicinally and used phrases like 'first-class digestive' and 'a good heart tonic' in their advertising campaigns. Those slogans herald from advertisements for 'White Horse', which also around this time became the first brand to use a screw-cap in place of a cork – sales doubled in a year following this innovation.

Prohibition, at the time, seemed like yet another disaster for the Scotch whisky industry, but of course it, unlike the vast majority of the bourbon distilleries, were able to continue producing stock. When Prohibition ended, the Scotch whisky industry was ready. The determination of the blenders to fulfil their customers' needs during that dark time was an effort

that would one day be richly rewarded by the American people.

In Scotland, DCL made various other purchases throughout the 1920s, and despite sitting in a position of great power, it would appear that under the watchful eyes of William Ross (the hero to Lloyd George's villain), took charge of the ongoing crisis with the greater good of the industry in mind by doing the only thing that it knew how – purchasing smaller operations when they were doomed to fail. It is thought by many that the careful steering conducted by DCL during this period contributed greatly towards the shape of the industry today.

The end of Prohibition and a drop in taxes gave new hope to the Scottish distilleries that had just about managed to weather the storm. But the wreckage from the previous 30 years was substantial. Only two of Campbeltown's 30+ distilleries remained in business. In addition to that, many of the Highland and Island distilleries had been hit hard, too, in favour of the delicate Speyside malts, again establishing the playing field for the present day.

The early 19th century saw the first mutterings of temperance in the United States. At first the movements, based out of Connecticut, Virginia and New York, advocated the restraint of alcohol consumption, but soon it turned into all-out abstinence. All alcoholic beverages were drawn into this, but spirits, and especially whiskey, were the primary target. The reasons that many people argued in favour of teetotalism were numerous. Much of the energy came from religious leaders, teachers, women's rights activists and women themselves, many of whom experienced the negative effects that alcohol had on their partners on a daily basis. This was reflected in largely women-based organisations, such as the Anti-Saloon League, who devised accompanying placards touting such phrases as:

'Lips that touch liquor shall not touch ours!'

For male and female members of the working class, alcohol had become a major part of everyday life and abstinence was a means of proving themselves worthy of the vote, a privilege that they were denied at the time. Temperance, it seemed, could solve these problems and much more.

Most of us consider 1919 as the beginning of Prohibition in America. It was in this year on January 16th that Nebraska became the 36th state to ratify the 18th amendment, and a year and a day later, the Volstead Act was put into effect. But in truth, it was not the sudden and shocking event that many would have you believe. Numerous states experimented with prohibition and prohibitive measures throughout the 1800s and, by 1913, nine states were already committed to the prohibition of alcohol. Nationwide prohibition was a

dead certainty by this point – it just took a few more years for Congress to approve the submittal of an amendment to the constitution of the United States. It was the 18th amendment, which prohibited 'the manufacture, sale, or transportation of intoxicating liquors within, the importation thereof into, or the exportation thereof from the United States and all territory subject to the jurisdiction thereof for beverage purposes.' Everyone assumed Prohibition would be short-lived and many people simply laughed it off to begin with. Nobody expected it to go on for 13 years.

The effect on Kentucky was, needless to say, cataclysmic. Prohibition didn't just alter the lives of distillers and brewers, but also farmers, truck drivers, shipping companies, saloon keepers, and restaurateurs, as tax revenues dropped and the cost of policing increased.

Prohibition was designed to cure the ills of society by ridding it of the temptation associated with the evils of alcohol. Instead, it had the opposite effect. Crime soared and criminals built empires

RIGHT A 19th-century temperance pledge certificate, promising abstinence from alcohol consumption.

through the illegitimate importation and production of alcohol, along with other profitable criminal activities.

All except a handful of distilleries were forced to close their doors and in Kentucky alone, 59 whiskey distilleries were shut down between 1918 and 1919, including H. Sutherland in Bardstown, a distillery that had been in business since before America even gained its independence. The Buffalo Trace Distillery, which at the time was called 'Stagg', was one of a handful of exceptions and remained semi-operational during the 13-year period, firing up its stills on at least four occasions. The government seized control of 'concentration warehouses' that contained whiskey stocks and allowed the spirit to be bottled for medical purposes only. Some of the familiar brand names, like 'Old Grandad', appeared on pharmacists' shelves, albeit with dumbed-down branding and more of a 'drugstore' look about them. Doctors could prescribe whiskey to patients for a variety of illnesses and ailments. Some were no doubt keener than others, and I suspect that certain doctors were offered both the carrot and the stick in return for cooperation.

Despite distilleries like Stagg topping up stocks for the medical industry, the level of whiskey in warehouses dropped steadily over the years and the average age of the product increased. By the time

TOP LEFT Federal agents pour illegal liquor into a sewer during the Prohibition.

TOP RIGHT Bystanders attempt to catch in cups moonshine being poured out of a window by federal agents during a raid on an illegal still in 1925.

ABOVE After a raid on a private home that served as a distribution warehouse for illegal liquor, a federal agent carries boxes of whiskey to load into his car before disposing of them.

Prohibition ended, almost all of the pre-Prohibition stocks had been exhausted. Demand during Prohibition was high of course, and today pre-Prohibition bottles of bourbon are very rare indeed. Any stocks that might have remained in unpillaged warehouses were, by 1933, very old and would have been blended with unaged or very young whiskies as producers hurried to fill the marketplace with any legal product that they could.

Smuggling whisky into the USA during the 1920s became a big business for some. Canada, where alcohol remained legal, played a particularly important role, providing a steady flow of liquor, namely Canadian Club, to thirsty American people. At the height of Prohibition there were thought to be over 1,000 bottles of Canadian Club crossing the US border every day. The popularity of Canadian, Scotch and Irish whiskies in America today can be attributed to its availability at a time when no domestic products were on the market.

The moonshiners were named after their preferred practice of night-time distilling, lit only by the light of the glowing moon. Ignoring for now the fact that the liquor was unquestionably low in quality and more than likely quite dangerous, the romance associated with moonshining is undeniable.

Ever since whiskey had been taxed, moonshining had been going on, but when Prohibition took effect, many farmers acknowledged the threat of poverty and did what they could to stay afloat. In other words, they turned anything fermentable into liquor. Moonshining went on all over America, but was endemic to states like Indiana, Virginia and Kentucky. In risking it all for distillation, these men became very resourceful at concealing their operations and making a quick getaway when the circumstances required it. Distillery set-ups were often designed to be loaded and unloaded quickly, and moonshiners used back roads and souped-up vehicles to transport their cargo from state to state. Fast and fearless drivers were prized for their abilities to outrun the cops, including Junior Johnson, who was never caught despite many years of transporting bootleg liquor at very high speed. After Prohibition ended, he transferred his formidable skills to professional motorsports driving and became a NASCAR legend.

Moonshining was dangerous in many ways, but perhaps none more so than in the act of drinking the stuff. Even unadulterated products were risky, due to the presence of methanol and higher-proof alcohols. Some moonshiners coloured their hooch with iodine and tobacco in efforts to pseudo-age the liquor. One report from New York in 1926 found that of the 576,000 gallons of moonshine seized that year, all contained traces of poisonous ingredients.

For a Cold

OLD Overholt Rye and quinine is an unfailing remedy in curing colds and preventing serious developments.

Old Overholt Rye

"Same for 100 years"

proves invaluable and saves many a doctor's bill. It possesses decidedly strengthening qualities and should be in the home, at all times, for emergencies. Aged in the wood, bottled in bond.

A. Overholt & Co., Pittsburgh, Pa.

LEFT A magazine advert in the 1930s extolling the health benefits of Old Overholt Rye, the brand that became the 'medicinal alcohol' used by the US Navy during World War II.

In New York alone there were up to 40 moonshine-related deaths a day during the 1920s.

The 'Noble Experiment', as Prohibition is often referred to, was ultimately a failure. Crime rates went up and criminals got rich; it ravaged the economy, created civil unrest, lowered government tax revenues and caused unemployment to skyrocket, hitting an all time high of 23.6% in 1932.

ABOVE Izzy Einstein (left) sharing a toast with his partner Moe Smith in a New York bar in 1935. In the 1920s, Izzy and Moe were the most effective team of Prohibition agents, using disguises to arrest bootleggers, close speakeasies and dispose of illegal liquor.

BELOW Unloading a consignment of newly legal whiskey after the end of the Prohibition in 1933.

THE TWENTIETH CENTURY AND BEYOND

The Great Depression of the 1930s trimmed Scotch production to an all-time low, forcing all but Glenlivet and Glen Grant to close. The end of Prohibition signalled some changes, however, and despite rising taxes the industry grew strongly until World War II war hit. Taxes increased to fund the war effort and foreign barley shortages spelled another period of decline in sales and an increase in prices. The price of a bottle in 1946 was around twice that of a pre-war bottle. Taxes increased by another 30% in 1947, but as more barley became available, production increased at a furious rate. This can be put largely down to demand for Scotch from the US, who no doubt felt it only right to reward the supply of whisky through the Prohibition years. There was an emotional connection to Scotland too, fostered by the US servicemen who passed through Scotland during World War II, no doubt sampling the spirit of the Highlands.

Japan's whisky story really got going in October 1923. Shinjiro Torii, an experienced whisky merchant and wine maker, began building the Yamazaki distillery and employed 29-year-old Masataka Taketsuru as his distillery manager. Five years previously, Taketsuru had travelled to Glasgow where he had enrolled in a chemistry course at the University. The real reason for his trip to Scotland though was a more practical kind of chemistry. This young Japanese man intended to learn the specific secrets of Scotch whisky making. By the time he left Scotland to go home in November 1920, he was likely the most accomplished distiller in Japan; not to mention husband to a Scottish wife, Rita. The experience that Taketsuru brought with him not only established the blueprint for the Yamazaki distillery, but also formed the mantra for Japanese whisky production to this day. Upon his return to Japan, Taketsuru insisted that the

distillery be set up in north Japan, where the climate was most similar to Scotland. Torii, ever the pragmatist, preferred the transport links and clean waters that could be found near Osaka. Torii won the argument, for at least ten years anyway, at which time Taketsuru set his own distillery up on the Northern island of Hokkaido. These rival distilleries at Yamazaki and Yoichi formed the basis of the Japanese whisky industry and marked the origins of Suntory and Nikka.

Until the middle of the 20th century, nearly all of the whisky in Scotland was matured in ex-Sherry casks. It had been an excellent arrangement but Sherry was becoming unfashionable with consumers in Europe, as well as in the US and Asia (whilst whisky was gaining popularity) so supplies began to dwindle. Many producers turned to bourbon barrels, but there was not a great supply of these either, since Prohibition and World War II had more or less destroyed the American spirits industry. Larger distillers, and especially grain operations, are known to have filled casks at much higher strength to compensate for the lack of wood.

Thanks to the work of Walker's, Dewar's, Mackie's and Buchanan's, it was blended whisky that continued to lead the way, typically drunk with a splash of soda. This 'whisky highball' became an American staple in the 1950s. However, not to be outdone, the USSR made their mark in the international spirits world, with vodka, quietly absorbing a massive chunk of the market.

The response from Scotland was already on its way. Rather than tackle the vodka highball head on, a new plan of attack was required and, in effect, a new style of beverage was created – neat whisky. In 1963, Glenfiddich became the first distillery to market a 'straight' malt whisky. It was eight years old and packaged in the distinctive triangular bottle shape. The campaign focused on single malt as a well-kept secret of the Scots and great emphasis was placed on its history, location, ingredients and intensity of flavour. Glenlivet (arguably the definitive single malt) followed with similar marketing campaigns for their own single malt, along with Glen Grant and Macallan. The single malt market was still tiny compared to that of blends, but a trickle-down effect was hoped for – something that would re-ignite the enthusiasm that had existed for the blends.

The American spirits industry watched the events unfolding in Scotland with great interest. The single malt posed a threat to their bourbon market, which had enjoyed steady growth since the war. A competitive edge was needed and it announced itself in the form of a single barrel. Single barrel bourbons were of course, not new; the likelihood is in fact that many of the earliest aged whiskies were not blended at all, but bottled directly from the cask. But Elmer T. Lee of the Buffalo Trace distillery (then Age International) remembered Colonel Albert Blanton, a former manager of the distillery in the 1930s (then Schenley) had, on occasion, bottled the liquid from exceptional barrels as special gifts. Lee bottled the first Blanton's Single Barrel Bourbon in 1984. With an emphasis on the single, it was closely followed by a Maker's Mark bottling and was the perfect counterattack to the growing single malt whisky that was being bottled across the pond. These products did especially well in Japan and quickly encouraged other producers to expand their range of bottlings. In turn, the small batch was born too, placing emphasis on the craft of the blender, who would use a comparatively small selection of barrels to blend a specific flavour profile that typically has an older average age and is higher in strength than standard labels.

RIGHT Today single malt whiskies and single barrel bourbons are produced all over the world, from Scotland and the USA to Japan.

Jim Beam got in there early in the late 1980s and early 1990s, launching in quick succession Basil Hayden's, Booker's, Baker's and Knob Creek. Heaven Hill had already launched their Elijah Craig brand by 1986. Not only did these high-end products add additional strings to the bourbon bow, but they also encouraged consumers to give the producers' core expressions (Jim Beam White label, for example) a second look.

In Japan, Keizo Saji, the second son of Shinjiro Torii, became president of his father's company in 1961. Saji is the man responsible both for propelling Suntory into its current stratospheric status, and for being the original driving force behind Japanese single malt whisky. Saji launched Yamazaki 12 in 1984 and at the time it was the first mass-marketed single malt around.

Meanwhile, Scotch whisky producers trudged on blindly into the dark, over-optimistic and blissfully ignorant to the impending downturn, as more and more drinkers turned their noses up at the prospect of the old man's drink. Overproduction ensued throughout the 1970s and 1980s and something had to give. In a repeat of what had happened in the 1920s, over 20 distilleries closed down in the years between 1981 and 1996, including legendary operations like Brora, Port Ellen and Rosebank.

Whisky's ability to adapt and evolve, to duck and dive, has enabled it to weather this latest storm as a more versatile and self-aware product. Whisky today understands its market, demands mass appeal and affords its drinkers an immense range of choice through different producing countries, distilleries, production methods and people.

Ultimately it is the whisky highball that commands the lion's share of whisky sales around the world today. I have for a long time believed that the younger generation will embrace the drinks their grandparents enjoyed and eschew the favourite drinks of their parents – it's a rebellion thing. The highball of the 1950s lives on, but in various shapes and forms, each dictated by local flavours and preference, but each steered by the common theme of whisky. Hipsters have shunned the grape-based products of their parents and turned to whisky and coke (as well as gin and tonic) as their choice-refreshment. In China and you'll find whisky mixed with green tea; in Japan it's often mixed with lots of cold water and increasingly with food. In Latin America, whisky is mixed with coconut water and in South Africa you'll find it partnered with Appletiser. The UK consumes almost half of all the world's Jack Daniel's... with coke, of course. These kind of drinks allow the blends and bourbons to do what they do best, integrate, accentuate and stimulate, resulting in a drink that is greater than the sum of its parts.

It's good news for single malt whisky too, where developed markets continue to demand a greater range of bottlings and producers are only too happy to fulfil the request at increasingly higher prices. Single Malt has become a vessel for celebration in countries like Russia,

Taiwan and Japan, the latter of which are doing a very good job of producing their own stocks of top-quality malt.

As I write, malt whisky is being made in over 25 countries around the world, including almost every country in Western Europe, Australia, New Zealand, South Africa, Pakistan, India and even Argentina. On top of that, five of the top ten fastest growing global spirits brands in 2012 were whisky products.

BELOW The St. George Distillery in California is a striking contrast between clinical steel architecture and warm copper distillation apparatus.

Most people will tell you that whisky is a product made from only three ingredients: cereal, water and yeast. I would argue that wood deserves a place on that list, too, since it is the influence of wood that provides the larger part of whisky's character. For some whiskies, most notably those from Scotland, there is arguably a fifth ingredient in the form of peat smoke, which can be a major flavour player in the finished product. Others may contest that the people who make whisky actually constitute an ingredient; after all it's their knowledge and experience that shape the character of the product. While I agree that people are critical to every stage of whisky production, from growing the cereals, right through to blending and bottling, I see them rather like ice in a cocktail: an integral and intrinsic part of the process, but a means to an outcome rather than a component of it.

The exciting thing about whisky making is that every stage of the process is meaningful and directly impacts the next stage. Of the four ingredients, wood is by far the most complex and unequivocally the most important. It is so familiar to us, yet somehow cryptic and arcane in its interaction with spirits. What we know for sure is that whisky gets a good proportion of its flavour and all of its colour from time spent encased in wood – without it we'd all be drinking white spirit and pulling strange faces.

Cereals are important, too, at least in the sense that they provide the energy source required to make alcohol in the first instance, and at most for the mouthfeel and lingering finish that they can contribute; the type of cereal used, be it malted barley, corn, rye, or wheat, does impart some flavour and textural nuances to the whisky. Bourbon sometimes has a sweet, popcorn-like quality, partly due to its 'mash-bill' (the proportion of different grains used during the mashing process), of which corn forms the majority. Rye

produces a dry, nutty, pepper-like character, and malt whisky a fruity, breakfast-cereal tone that underpins the other goings-on. However, detecting the mash bill of a Bourbon in blind tasting is not always straightforward, since many other factors come into play. Assessing whether a 20-year-old grain whisky is made from corn or wheat is no easier. For this reason, cereal is important from a practical point of view, but still limited in its contribution to the character of the final product.

Water, while crucial for virtually every stage of the whisky-making process, is not something that we should get too excited about or romance over. Assuming that the water is of acceptable quality and free from excessive bacteria or pollution, a distillery only needs to meet a limited number of parameters for the water to do its job. Pay no heed to talk of artesian wells and 1,000-year-old springs; it has little to do with the final product.

Yeast is the hardest ingredient of the four for us to relate to, and yet one of the more influential, in my opinion. Microscopic and numerous, it's only recently that distillers have begun to accept that the type of yeast can have a lasting impact on the character of the bottle. We don't hear much about yeast in day-to-day life, however; arousing excitement over a discussion centred around yeast culture is a luxury reserved only for the geekiest of whisky geeks.

Besides the raw ingredients that provide whisky with its substance and mass, there are various tools and techniques that also shape the final outcome. Like wood, many of these practices straddle the void of mysticism that connects our world and that of the whisky gods. Many of the older whisky distilleries of the world are heavily laden with superstition and supposition; 'turn that knob first' and 'clean that vat last' are calls that can be heard not in the pursuit of correct practice, but in the adherence to ritual. Much has been learned through scientific pursuit, but many unexpected outcomes still leave whisky makers scratching their heads and pondering the unfathomable.

In the following chapters, we'll take an in-depth look into what whisky is made from and how it is made, covering each stage in sufficient detail to understand the state of the liquid in our glass. Here we go...

WATER

I was always led to believe that the whiskies of Scotland and whiskies from other parts of the world owed much of their character and style to their immediate surroundings and their water. As one of the four ingredients used to make whisky, and perhaps the one that we associate with the easiest, it's not surprising that many brands and whisky books have placed a great deal of emphasis on water-sourcing in the past; the brands, in particular, have enjoyed showering us with creative descriptions of how and where their water has been obtained – hand-extracted from the crystal ice-clouds of Tibet's most inaccessible subterranean diamond palace, for example (alright, I made that one up). Likewise, I have read well-respected whisky books that stress how many whiskies owe much of their character to water filtered through 'granite mountains' and 'sandstone stacks', or water sourced from 'ancient lakes'. One book even features a water heading under each distillery, complete with a life history of the water source. But around five years ago the veil of mystery that shrouded the subject of distillery water was lifted for me, when my friend Stuart Howe, one of the world's most accomplished brewers, told me that he could add and remove minerals from his water so as to emulate naturally occurring water from anywhere in the world. I was shocked and slightly concerned by his unholy claim, having been led to believe that good-quality, natural water was the backbone of any great brewing or distilling operation. But the more I investigated, the more I found that many distilleries were modifying their water sources to fit their needs. And in my opinion, it makes total sense to do so.

BELOW The River Spey in northeastern Scotland. Good for Salmon fishing and good for whisky, it's Scotland's fastest-flowing river, and the setting for almost half of its distilleries.

Sure, 200 years ago, a good water source was one of the major considerations when deciding upon a distillery's location, principally because water powered the wheels of the mill, which was used to grind down the cereals ready for mashing. Nowadays, the water used to make whisky is still of critical importance to the manufacturing process – it's used in every single stage of whisky production, from irrigating crops to malting, mashing, distilling and bottling, and by my estimates it takes around 50 litres/53 quarts of 'process water' to make 1 litre/quart of whisky (and that doesn't include the water used for the various stages of cooling and cleaning that take place along the way) – but it's actually of very little consequence in terms of where it comes from. Most distilleries use tap water, while some utilize spring water.

Bourbon distillers in Kentucky have long claimed that their water, which passes through limestone, has a certain quality about it that is important to their product. Maker's Mark is one such brand that places great emphasis on the ecology of the area surrounding its water source. On the other hand, Brown-Forman, which produces Woodford Reserve, will tell you that the type of water is not an important part of its product. Harold Ferguson, the veteran distiller of Canadian Mist, once said: 'I'd choose to make whisky out of the cleanest water I could get. You can adjust everything else.'

Thankfully it's becoming rarer to hear whisky makers ramble on about their water source. I put this down to two factors, firstly because many of them simply use the tap water, and secondly because consumer understanding has improved to the point that two much more significant factors determining whisky flavour – wood and still shape – are attracting greater interest.

Using water from the tap/faucet might sound less romantic, but it makes perfect sense, because it's a very consistent supply that has already met various quality standards. Once it arrives, it is further processed to the requirements of the distillery, which means checking levels of copper and iron, stripping out chlorine and even adding minerals like zinc, calcium and magnesium that help promote enzyme activation in mashing and ensure a healthy fermentation process.

Before farming, the human race was stuck in a rut. The acts of eating and drinking were hardly ever planned more than a few days in advance and we generally munched on whatever we were capable of catching or snatching. One day, however, around 15,000 years ago, it became clear to our ancestors that something had to be done. Food seemed to be fairly essential for life and we needed more of it to avoid the repetitive nomadic stresses of migration and death by starvation (or sabre-toothed cat). So crops were purposely planted, domesticated and nurtured, the first of which were cereals, the edible seeds or grains of the grass family Gramineae. Barley or wheat were probably the first, sewn in the 'Fertile Crescent' of the Middle East, which later went on to become the Mesopotamian Empire. Farming, the world's second-oldest profession, had been born.

Eating cereals straight from the fields is no one's idea of a fun day out, though – they're tough, difficult to chew and digest, and almost flavourless. So history's first chefs and bartenders set about developing a menu of dishes that would both satisfy the stomach and please the palate. Water was found to be a good medium for softening the hard structure of the grain, and if heated, a kind of porridge or gruel would form. Bring some naturally occurring yeast into the fold, and you have the ingredients for two of life's most important things – bread and beer.

Evidence of cereal fermentation goes back around 8,000 years, but the earliest written record of brewing beer comes from the Sumerian Empire around 6,000 years ago. The Sumerians loved beer; it's even mentioned in their (and the world's) oldest story

– *The Epic of Gilgamesh*. In the story, the bestial giant Enkidu consumed beer, shed his fur, danced and became a human. Enkidu became a metaphor for man's progress towards civilization through the merits of beer. Indeed, so precious were the building blocks of beer to prehistoric man that grain stores essentially operated like banks.

THE DIFFERENT GRAINS

Grain cereals fall into one of two categories: warm-season crops, like corn and millet, and cold-season crops, like barley, oats, rye and wheat. They are all packed with carbohydrates in the form of starch, a potent little package of energy that the plant uses to germinate and grow. It's generally accepted that the variety within the sub-family of cereal has little effect on the flavour of the final product. Indeed, by the time the grain has gone through malting, mashing, fermenting, distillation (at least twice), ageing, filtering and bottling, it would be a difficult case to argue – like insisting that the quality of the cattle feed affects the smell of the leather. Having said that, many distillers believe that the variety of the grain can be responsible for oiliness, waxy qualities and thickness on the palate.

While flavour may not be a concern, the specific cereal variety does affect the yield of alcohol, which in turn affects the amount of money that can be made from it – in this, all distillers are united. Each type of grain poses different challenges in its processing, too – see page 64 for more on this.

BARLEY

There are, apparently, over 300,000 varieties of barley in the world – so many that it strikes me that one person would not be able to count them all. Barley's excuse is that it's a type of grass, and grasses have a propensity for mutation. Barley used for malting accounts for only a small percentage of the total, but a staggering 25% of the world's total supply of barley is malted, mostly for the production of alcoholic beverages.

Barley comes in two distinct forms, 'two-row' and 'six-row', which are identifiably different because the former has two rows of seed on each spike (head), whereas the latter has six rows of seed on each spike. Scotch distillers prefer two-row, because it's typically lower in protein and produces a higher yield of fermentable sugars. In the USA, six-row barley is preferred, since it typically contains more enzymes, which are necessary for their corn- and rye-rich mash bills (see page 54 and 64–65).

The Old English word for barley is bære, and one of the earliest varieties of barley grown in Scotland is an old heritage crop called bere, a six-row barley derived from the same word. Bere is thought to be the root origin of the word 'barn' and these days, it is only grown on the island of Orkney. Highland Park, one of two distilleries on Orkney (the other is Scapa) used bere up until 1929. Young upstart distillery Arran and Bruichladdich have recently launched special release bere malts. You can still buy bere bannock, a kind of flatbread made from the bere grown on Orkney. For making spirits, bere is not a sensible choice, though. Over the past 200 years new strains of barley have been cultivated that are more resilient to disease – and to the Scottish climate. What's more, they are easier to process, and produce a higher yield of alcohol per ton.

In the mid-19th century, a typical malt distillery would turn 1 bushel (8 gallons/9½ US gallons) of malted Archer or Goldthorpe barley into 2 gallons/2½ US gallons) of spirit. A hundred years later, the same weight of hybrid barleys, Spratt-Archer or Plummage-Archer, would be enough to produce 3 gallons/3½ US gallons of spirit (note: these volumes are of 'potable' spirit, not pure alcohol – by today's standards, you need roughly 1kg/2 lbs. 4oz. of barley to make a 70cl/24 fl. oz. bottle of whisky). These improvements in yield can also be partly attributed to

ABOVE Barley really is the brick that builds many of the towering whiskies that we know and love.

better production methodology and machinery, but over the past 50 years, yield has increased by 30%, while practices have remained relatively unchanged. The introduction of the Golden Promise barley variety in 1968 marked a huge leap forward for the industry, as it matured early and thrived in the Scottish climate; 10 years later more than 90% of the malting barley used in Scotland came from Scottish-grown Golden Promise.

Golden Promise has, in turn, been surpassed; given the economic rewards involved, it's not surprising to hear that new varieties are still being developed today. Think about it: even a variety capable of producing 1% equates to tens of millions of pounds worth of additional spirit. At the time of writing, Optic and Decanter lead the way, but keep an eye out for next-generation varieties like Odyssey and Chronicle stealing the limelight soon.

All barley is air-dried after harvest, taking its moisture content from 20% to 12%. Next, it is graded for size and cleaned, then cooled over a period of months from 20°C (68°F) to 5°C (41°F). This temperature change causes the grain to start preserving itself, ready for us to trick it into thinking it's in the ground and warm, ready for germination. During its time spent in the storage facility, ventilation and condensation are closely monitored to prevent the onset of mildew.

WHEAT

Wheat is highly adaptable and numerous in its varieties, having been domesticated for at least as long as barley. It can be planted as a winter or spring crop, and as such, crops up a lot all over the world. The alcohol industry uses winter wheat almost exclusively, since it has a higher starch content and produces more alcohol per bushel. The spring wheat tends to be used for bread making, since it has the desirable higher protein content.

Most grain whiskies produced in Scotland are made from wheat (corn lost favour in the 1980s) and wheat makes up a portion of the mash bill in some American whiskies, too. Wheat was the choice grain for Canadian whiskies back in the early-1800s, but most distilleries have switched to corn now for their 'bulk alcohol' requirements.

Wheat produces a smooth distillate that adds sweetness and a mellow characteristic that tempers the harshness that can come from corn and rye. Think about Belgian wheat beers, with their silky, delicate character, and you'll have a good idea of the contribution wheat makes to whisky.

CORN (MAIZE)

Corn, or maize, is indigenous to the warm climates of Central America, and was probably first domesticated around 2,500 BC. Native Americans relied heavily on corn, which actually featured in some of their religious practices, and were quick to convert forested areas into plantations. To this day, it makes up a huge proportion of the Mexican and Central American diet. It is also the one truly American ingredient in American whiskies.

Native Americans first showed settlers how to cultivate corn, and today it is the most widely grown crop throughout the USA and Americas, accounting for half of the world's production, with over one-third of that being used to make alcohol. Three of the top corn-growing states in the USA also have something else in common, in that they all begin with 'I' – Iowa, Indiana and Illinois.

The variety of corn used in the production of American whiskey is 'dent' corn, which can be easily identified by the dent in the crown of the kernel. Interestingly, corn is the one truly American ingredient used to make American whiskies. It gives a higher yield of alcohol than the other cereals mentioned here, due to its high sugar and starch content. It's also quite easy to work with, lacking some of the compounds that can cause other cereals to turn into porridge or glue. Corn makes up the majority of the mash bill in bourbon, and, when doing its job properly, contributes all the sweet and buttery characteristics we expect from popcorn. If allowed to dominate, the spirit can become greasy and thin – think excessively buttered popcorn.

Corn was the primary cereal used in Scottish grain whisky until the mid-1980s, when competitively priced wheat began to take over. Until the 1980s, most of the corn was imported from the USA, but these days it is typically sourced from the warm areas of southern France.

Corn grows on the familiar 'cob' structure, with each cob holding up to 1,000 corn seeds, of which around 85% is starch. Corn is harvested at the end of the summer, just as the kernels are beginning to dry out. After harvesting they are dried further, down to a moisture content of approximately 14%.

RYE

Rye is the delicious cockroach of the cereal world. It's both tenacious and hardy, and more than capable of growing in snow-covered Eastern Europe and in soils that no other cereal would survive in. Rye is a fully fledged winter crop, usually sewn in the autumn and harvested in the early summer. It is covered with a husk and a 'beard', and grains are arranged in an alternating pattern along the rachis (a zig zag-shaped stalk). If a wheat grain is the fat thumb of a baker, rye is the slender index finger of a pâtissier.

Rye is characterful and complex as an ingredient in bread, beer or whisky, but many farmers don't grow it because it's not very lucrative. Beer and spirit producers avoid it because it has a powerful flavour and it's a bit of a nightmare to brew with, as it has the absorbency of a sponge, and features particularly high levels of a starch group called beta-glucan, which means that brewing a rye-heavy wash can feel a bit like cooking a pot of bubblegum. I've heard stories of enterprising distillers using their sticky rye mash to plug holes in their stills!

In North America, where it is used to make rye whiskey and, in the past, Canadian whisky (which is sometimes referred to simply as 'rye') the crop grows in the cooler northern states like the Dakotas and Minnesota and in various parts of Canada. It makes sense, as these areas best match the cool Eastern Europe climates from which the grain originated.

Character is where rye comes into its own. In many bourbon mash bills, rye is used to add an element of pepperiness and dryness that balances the sweet, oily, corn. Bourbon without rye can be a bit flabby and gutless, while rye whiskey itself (which contains a minimum of 51% rye) is full of all that engine-oil heat and raw-bran nuttiness.

THE WHISKY PRODUCTION PROCESS

	MALT WHISKY		IRISH WHISKEY		
Grain	Barley				
Malting	Malting				
Kiln	Unpeated or peated drying				
Milling	Ground down to grist		Milled with malted barley		
Mashing	Sent to mash tun for mashing with water at 63.5°C (146.3°F)		Mashing at 55°C (131°F), rising to 65°C (149°F) and finally 75°C (167°F)		
Addition					
Fermentation	50–100 hours		60–120 hours		
Distillation	1st: Copper wash still 2nd: Copper spirits still		Any combination of pot and column still	1st pot still	
	3rd/additional distillation	No additional distillation		2nd pot still	
				3rd pot still	
Filtering					
Maturation	Refill cask	Ex-bourbon cask	Ex-Sherry cask		
	Finishing in wine cask or no finishing				
Water	Added to adjust strength				
Filtering	Chill-filtered				
Colour adjusted	Caramel (E150)				

GRAIN WHISKY		BOURBON, TENNESSEE & RYE	
Any (typically wheat)		Any (predominantly corn & rye)	
Sometimes		Milled	
Cooking		Corn is cooked at a high temperature	
		No other cereals added (Bourbon and Tennessee)	Rye and/or wheat added at lower temperature
		Malted barley added	
		Sour mash/set-back added	
48 hours		Fermented without filtering for 3–5 days	
Column-still distillation		Single column distillation	
Additional column distillation	No additional columns	Thumper (only used at Early Times and Bernheim distilleries)	Doubler
		Maple charcoal filtered (Tennessee)	
Matured in ex-bourbon casks		Cut to no more than 62.5% ABV and matured in new charred American oak casks	
Natural cask strength			
Non-chill-filtered			
No caramel		None permitted	

Malting is the transformation of a grain from a lifeless seed to an energetic sack of potential. All cereals are capable of being malted, but barley is by far the best. Barley contains a higher concentration of *diastase* (a family of enzymes) that is necessary to facilitate the malting process. The aim of malting is to prepare the grain for releasing its starch, and to liberate the *diastatic* power that converts the starches into simple sugars during mashing. Once successfully malted, the barley can be mashed on its own (as when producing malt whisky), or it can be mixed with other cereals, like corn, rye or wheat (as with bourbon, rye, Canadian whisky and Irish whiskey), where it will provide the enzymes needed to break down the other cereals' starches, too.

All cereals have structural similarities and contain an embryo (the brains) and an endosperm (the muscle). The first stage in the growth of a barley embryo involves the embryo's hormones triggering the release of enzymes that self-destruct cell walls and proteins, and ready the grain for breaking down starch stored in the endosperm into simpler sugars. If occurring naturally, this process gives the plant enough fuel to power growth until it can draw energy from the nutrients in the soil.

I once had the malting process explained to me in the context of a hazelnut chocolate bar, where the hazelnuts represented the starch. The wrapper represents the protein matrix that holds all of the cells of the plant in place. During malting, the protein is first broken down – the chocolate bar is unwrapped. Next, the individual cells are separated from one another – the chocolate bar is broken into segments. Finally, the enzymes break down the cell structure, revealing the starch – the chocolate is peeled away, leaving only the nuts.

Malting is essentially a clever growth mechanism that protects the grain's energy store until such time that it is

ABOVE Tiny rootlets emerge from a handful of 'green malt', indicating that the process is complete and the barley is now ready for drying.

RIGHT Yours truly attempting to turn malt in the traditional manner at the Benriach distillery in Speyside. Even a couple of minutes is exhausting, which led me to the conclusion that maltmen truly are men of steel!

needed. What the naive barley grain didn't plan for, though, is us. Through our mastery of all things botanical we have learned to trick the barley grain into believing that it's time to grow, opening the gates to its treasury and allowing us to raid the coffers. The secret to good malting is controlling the trickery, giving the grain all the encouragement it needs, then stopping it in its tracks before it has a chance to use its resources. What's left behind is an energy-rich package, ready for mashing and fermentation.

Most distilleries around the world buy in their malted barley from a commercial malting facility, prepared to their required grain size, nitrogen content (and indicator of starch content) and moisture levels – all important factors to determine spirit yield and, some would say, flavour. Commercially malted barley is produced on a huge scale, with state-of-the-art equipment, ensuring consistency and quality. Some Scottish distilleries, however, (six at the time of writing) still malt a proportion of the barley they use in the

traditional manner. Springbank is the only distillery that malts all of its own barley. Kilchoman has recently released its 100% Islay expression, where the barley is both grown and malted in its own facility. This is not without its headaches, though. Temperature control, good timing and a committed labour force are required to manage traditional floor maltings, but the romance and craft associated with the process are a big draw for many whisky drinkers.

STEEPING

The first stage of malting is the steep. Here, the dried grains are soaked in cold water for around 36–48 hours. The water is drained and refreshed a few times and oxygen is bubbled through it. These are the ideal conditions to trick the barley into germinating, as it believes that its surroundings are being subjected to natural rainfall. During this time, the grains will go from 12%–45% water content. Much is often made of the type of water used during this stage, with romantics favouring water percolating through peat bogs, but it makes no difference at all. Barley naturally filters the water, removing contaminants along the way.

GERMINATION

In traditional floor malting, the plump grains are taken from the steeps and spread across malting floors, typically 30cm/12 inches in depth. It's at this stage that a piece of genetic code within the barley whips the enzymes (diastase) into action, and biomechanical reactions begin to take place at a vigorous pace. Protein structure and cell walls are broken down, allowing access to the inner sanctum of starch, which is converted into its soluble form, dextrin, by the enzyme amylase. Moisture levels must be maintained to

BELOW LEFT Barley is added to large vessels called steeps, containing water. Growth starts as the grains absorb water.

BELOW RIGHT A grain of barley appears dull and lifeless on the surface, but hormones and enzymes are busy at work.

ABOVE The large steeping vessels in this room, at Port Ellen Maltings on Islay in Scotland prepare the barley for malting. Here, we see the might of industry bend a knee to the humble barley grain, all in the pursuit of liberating its valuable sugar stocks.

keep the enzymes happy, and it's common to see maltmen checking the thermometers that protrude from the barley beds (16°C/61°F is the optimum malting temperature). They also test the sponginess (using their feet) and rake or shovel the malt (using a malt 'shiel') to prevent the clumping that occurs when rootlets emerge from the seed and grab hold of each other! This endless turning of the barley is the cause of a repetitive strain injury common to maltmen called 'monkey shoulder'; in 2005, William Grant launched an innovative blended whisky eponymous to the affliction. I'm also told that in the past, maltmen would keep one fingernail longer than the others (a bit like some Spanish guitarists), which would be used to break open the grain and check the growth.

Commercial malting takes place in either Saladin boxes or drum maltings. Both work in much the same way, with the speed of germination controlled by airflow that cools the heat produced during the process. The Saladin box is a huge circular or rectangular trough. The malting drum looks like a coffee roaster,

intermittently turning the grains and distributing the heat as the drum rotates. I was told by Ramsay Borthwick at Port Ellen Maltings that the temperature of the barley inside its drum malting once rose to 40°C/104°F when a power cut stopped the coolers from running. The barley was half-cooked by the time the power was restored.

An experienced maltman is able to tell when the malting is complete by feeling a single grain. The plant begins to draw energy from the shoot end first, noticeably by the softening of its structure. As the germination process continues, the plant softens right down to its tip, and once the whole thing can be squashed into a kind of mushy flour, it is deemed fully germinated.

KILN DRYING

Germination can take between four and 12 days, based on humidity, temperature and airflow. By this time, the grains have sprouted tiny rootlets, which look a bit like tadpoles. Once the rootlets reach about three-quarters of the length of the grain, the 'green malt' is sent for drying. The barley has now reached the perfect balance – its structure has been sufficiently broken down, but its energy source still remains intact. The biomechanical process must now be halted and the barley's endosperm killed.

Kiln drying is a balance between airflow and temperature control. Whether conducted in a commercial maltings or at the distillery itself, kiln drying is the simple process of blowing warm air up and through the bed of green malt. Most modern kilns are fuelled by coke, rather than coal, as it is a slightly cleaner (and non-toxic) fuel that gives off only water and carbon-dioxide as by-products.

At the start of the kiln drying process, the airflow will usually be stronger and the temperature lower, which encourages moisture to migrate from the inside of the grain to the outside. Slowly the temperature is increased from 40°C/104°F up to as high as 75°C/167°F and the airflow reduced; the whole process takes around 36 hours in a commercial maltings. Once dried down to 4% moisture, the barley must then be stored for a minimum of two months before being milled and mashed. The longer the better, too, as it gives the moisture content of the grain a chance to equalize, following the same principle as resting your Christmas turkey!

Many of the malt whisky distilleries of Scotland still feature one or more pagoda roofs, which pinpoint the location of the kiln room. The Daluaine Distillery's kiln room roof was originally designed by Charles Chree Doig in 1889, emulating the tiered roof towers of eastern Asia. The premise was simple – allow good airflow up from the kiln and stop rain from getting in and wetting the barley. Nearly all the pagoda roofs in Scotland are decorative features today, since only a handful of distilleries still malt their own barley. If you do spot a pagoda chimney on top of a building, it's highly likely that the place was once used as a maltings.

LEFT The pagoda-style chimney at Highland Park Distillery.

RIGHT Heavy peat 'reek' rises ascends up a chimney, imparting flavour into the barley above.

BELOW The kiln room at Highland Park: old, unchanged, and still very much in use.

⋙ PEAT ⋘

The Scots turned to peat as a fuel when it became apparent that they didn't have enough wood or coal to burn. Peat bogs are formed when plant roots, moss, heather and other vegetation decompose in an acidic environment without drainage. The vegetation eventually decomposes, because it's always wet, and over hundreds and thousands of years of crushing gravity, it forms a loose organic mass that, if dried, can be burned.

In the grand scheme of things peat is not a great fuel source. It comprises around 60% carbon, so it gives off far less heat than comparable fossil fuels – and it makes everything smell! But it's this smell that has enticed so many of us into the world of Scotch whisky. Just like barbecued food, there's something primal and fundamental about the intoxicating aroma of smoke. It feels like home.

CUTTING PEAT

Many years ago, I cut peat in Ireland with my father. I recall, on most occasions, being more than a little reluctant to participate in this soggy, cold and windswept practice, ironically designed to keep my grandmother's house warm. Cutting is usually done at the beginning of the summer, to give the rolls of peat time to dry out, ready for the cold winter months. There are three specialized tools that peat cutters use to lever their prize from the earth. First is a flat shovel that removes the top layer of soil; the second tool is something akin to a giant palette knife/metal spatula, which slices

downwards and levers the slab of peat out from underneath. Finally, there's a pitchfork that's used for collecting debris.

Cutting peat by hand is a little like deconstructing a house brick-by-brick – care and attention must be taken to ensure that the next layer down is preserved so that it can be cut out in uniform pieces. I'm told that an experienced peat cutter can 'win' up to 1,200 rolls of peat on a good day. It sounds like a lot, but in the cold winter climates of Scotland and Ireland, a single household could get through 50 rolls in a single day! If you're feeling thirsty after a long day peat cutting, the traditional refreshment is a choice mixture of uncooked oats and water – delicious.

There's no question that peat cutters are tough men. My friend and whisky expert Colin Dunn was once taken on a peat-cutting expedition on Islay. He noticed that a bottle of malt whisky was loaded into the peat cutter's bag, and an hour or so into slicing away at the ground, Colin was parched and ready for a wee dram. Eventually the peat cutter stopped his work, produced the bottle, pulled the cork and then proceeded to throw it over his shoulder. The man then turned to Colin and, with a glint in his eye, said 'Well… ye know what that means, don't ye?!'

When you bear in mind that peat was originally used to fire the stills of early malt makers in the 18th century, a considerable workforce must have been needed to cut enough peat to last the winter. I suppose it's possible that the peat smoke in these distilleries imparted a fragrant finish to the distillate, which soon became a sought-after quality. One way or another, peat was being used exclusively to dry barley by 1700. Logic tells us to expect some seriously peaty

LEFT Peat can be as soft as compost or hard, like clay, depending on where it came from and what depth it was dug.

whiskies from this era, but the truth is that many of the old samples that exist are not overpoweringly peaty. The reason for this remains a mystery to whisky historians. In my view, much of it comes down to science and the peat saturation threshold of the barley grain (see pages 62–63).

These days, most peat is often cut in a slightly less romantic fashion. Vast lengths of land are literally sawn open, the organic matter sucked out, then neatly displayed on the ground for drying. One method incorporates a modified digger shovel that acts like a giant egg slicer. Another sucks the peat out mechanically, leaving behind what looks a little like the fecal matter of several hundred elephants.

The density and composition of peat does vary based on the depth it is cut, the geology and local ecosystem of its origin. Talisker, for example, is thought to derive its slight salinity from the salty sea air and occasional spatter of seaweed to which its peat is exposed. Meanwhile, Highland Park uses only the top couple of layers of the peat bog, which feels more like soil and is rich with heather roots. Dig deeper and you'll be rewarded with a more carbonic peat that is more like coke or coal. The deeper, darker stuff, or 'black peat', contributes less phenolic flavour (see pages 62–63) than the 'brown peat' that is found closer to the surface. A

TOP Scarred land on Orkney, where Highland Park peat cutters have taken slices of flavoursome mud from the bog on Hobbister Moor.

ABOVE Dark smoke is preferred over paler, white smoke – a sign that the peat is impacting the maximum phenol effect onto the barley.

combination of both types can give the necessary heat as well as the phenolic aromatics that are required to dry and flavour the barley successfully.

THIS PAGE After the peat is cut by hand using specialized tools, the resulting 'sod' is left outside to dry in the open air for around 2–3 weeks. Following this, the peat is collected and then transported to the distillery.

HOW WHISKY IS MADE

� THE SCIENCE OF PEAT ⨞

Peat is possibly the only component of malt whisky production that is genuinely governed by terroir, but I am well aware that that statement may upset one or two people. The composition of peat smoke (aptly named 'reek') is made up various volatile compounds that give the familiar burnt mustiness of peat smoke, most notably phenols. Depending on the location and the depth of the cut, the compounds will differ. Ardmore in Speyside uses a carbon-rich peat that gives its whisky a light, 'sooty' quality that's in contrast to the more maritime and medicinal drams that you might find on Islay or the Isle of Skye.

The peatiness of a whisky is measured in phenolic parts per million (ppm). By definition this means that a whisky of 1ppm would contain one phenolic molecule for every 999,999 other molecules. The most heavily peated whisky currently available is Octomore, produced by Bruichladdich; at 169ppm it's enough to make you cough just thinking about it.

The level of peatiness in the final product is nearly impossible to control during kilning – there are simply too many intangibles. These range from the exact moisture of the barley to the make-up of the peat itself, and how well the peat fire has been tended. A gauge can be taken by looking at the quality and density of the smoke, but that's about it. When tending a kiln you will be looking for rich, dark smoke rather than pale, white smoke, a sign that it contains plenty of phenols. Fire is not your friend, as the more delicate aromatics can be lost if the peat gets too hot. In a good kiln, you should be able to touch the peat while it's smoking without burning your hands.

And then there's the break point, which occurs about halfway through kilning (at roughly 18 hours). This marks the stage where the barley will accept no more phenolic compounds, as a result of its ever-decreasing moisture content. Pre-break, there is plenty of moist air and the damp husk of the barley absorbs phenols like a sponge, but as the grain dries out, so too does its capacity for trapping the peat characteristics. After the break point, the air becomes drier and no amount of peat will increase its ppm any further.

Port Ellen Maltings on Islay always burn approximately 10 tons of peat for every 50 tons of barley, and the results range from as low as 30ppm right up to 80ppm. In commercial kilning, a sample of peated barley is taken after the kilning process and its ppm is measured. The batches are then blended together to create an average ppm at the desired level.

Of course, the phenolic parts in peated barley won't all make it through to the bottle. Despite being resilient little beasts, the phenols have to undergo the trials of mashing, fermentation, distillation and ageing. For example, Laphroaig peats its barley to 40ppm, its new-make spirit is 25ppm, but its finished whiskies are all below 10ppm.

It's also worth noting that the phenolic parts per million in a whisky are only a guideline to how smoky a whisky will really be when you come to taste it. Although it's possible to measure phenols accurately, the ppm does not account for other flavourful molecules that might combat the smokiness and lessen our perception of it.

RIGHT Commercial maltings produce over 99% of the malted barley needed to make whisky.

MILLING AND MASHING

MILLING

Before mashing can take place, the grains must first be milled down to size. In the case of barley, this increases surface area, but also separates the husk from the innards, allowing better conversion rates (from starch to sugar) and turning the husks into a useful filtering system that stops tiny particles draining out of the wash later down the line. Whole (split) husks are preferred as they offer a better medium for efficient percolation. For other grains like corn, wheat and rye, the milling similarly increases surface area, but also gives better access to the starch stores. Many American distilleries use a type of 'hammer' mill to powder their cereals, which pretty much does what it says on the tin and pounds the grains into a fine powder using rotating hammers – ouch! Particle size is of critical importance during mashing and fermentation, and can have a big impact on the final alcohol yield. Never underestimate the mill. Having said that, I have seen evidence to suggest that one or two grain distilleries in the UK don't actually mill at all, and instead they promote longer cooking times of their wholegrains to extract the necessary starch.

In the case of malt whisky, the malt is milled down to a flaky powder called grist, and no other cereals are added. In contrast, the malted barley proportion of a typical bourbon or rye mash bill is usually about 5–15%. Irish pot still whiskey can be made up of between 40–100% malted barley, with the rest being unmalted barley.

MASHING

Mashing is a crucial stage in the pursuit of fermentable sugars before fermentation. This is where the ground-down cereals are mashed and heated with water, which converts their starch into

sugars, resulting in a sweet liquid called wort, which is better known as unfermented beer.

Starches are ungainly things made up of connecting chains of glucose molecules. For fermentation to work, these starches need to be broken down into more simple sugars so that the yeast can successfully 'feed' on them. During mashing, our arsenal of enzymes that were gathered during malting target starches in the mash and break them down into simple sugars.

For malt whisky, the barley is added to a mash tun mashed into hot water at 69°C/156°F, which subsequently drops to around 64°C/147°F, known as the strike point. This temperature must be maintained precisely to get the maximum levels of fermentable sugar out of the malt without damaging the enzymes. After about an hour, the wort is drained off through a mesh called a lauter screen, which filters out the husks and solids, and is then sent on to the washback for fermentation. A second and third mashing takes place to extract the maximum amount of sugar from the remaining grist. This involves increasing the mashing temperature up to 70°C/158°F and 88°C/190°F, respectively. The final (third) mash extracts very little sugar, and is known as sparge, leaving behind the spent grist. This water is then used as part of the first water on the next mash. This is standard for most distilleries, although some get away with using only two sets of water and a 'continuous sparge', like Caol Ila; others use four sets of water, like Springbank.

For American whiskey, the non-malt cereals (corn, rye, wheat) are cooked first to gelatinize the starch, preparing them for the addition of the malt later on. Corn, in particular, has to be boiled at 100°C/212°F, which causes the starch to swell irreversibly, breaking hydrogen bonds, and causing no end of disruption to the starch matrix. Some distilleries, like Four Roses, do this in a massive pressure cooker. These beasts can heat the mash up to over 130°C/266°F, which can dramatically speed up the process. Other producers use a slightly less efficient steaming method, which is thought to be a little more gentle on the product. Rye is cooked at 78°C/172°F and malted barley and wheat at around 65°C/149°F. The whole thing is a bit like making a casserole, where all the different ingredients must be cooked to different temperatures and times for them to be at their best. One of the main differences between mashing and fermenting American whiskey compared to malt whisky, is the fact that the mash is not filtered in between the two stages.

Before production was scaled up, the mashmen of America used to do all their mashing and fermenting in standard wooden barrels. They would add their mash bill to a cask containing hot water and give it a good stir with a long paddle.

ABOVE These old mills are a common sight in Scottish distilleries; they were constructed so well that modern mills are a surprising rarity in this part of the world.

LEFT The 115-year-old mash tun at Edradour still retains its original cast iron floor and walls, and would be difficult to replicate using modern techniques.

THIS PAGE Mashing is a careful balance between
the ratio of ingredients, temperature of water
and milling of cereals, with the ultimate goal of
converting as much starch into sugar as possible.

FERMENTATION

Yeast is a microscopic single-celled organism that exists all around us and on virtually everything we touch. It's on the pages of the book you're reading now, in the air you're breathing, and even working away inside your digestive system. You can only see yeast cells under a microscope and to give you an idea of their size, you will find approximately 100 million test cells in a single 7g/¼oz. packet of baker's yeast that you find in a supermarket or grocery store. If you leave a covered bowl of flour and water out for a couple of days, you will see it begin to bubble and come alive. Microscopic yeast cells, descended from the air but also present on the flour itself, devour the food source, multiply in numbers, and pump out carbon dioxide and alcohol.

When yeast is added to a sugary wort (beer), three actions take place: firstly, the yeast multiplies by using the sugar to form new cell material. Secondly, the yeast 'ferments' – an anaerobic reaction involving the breakdown of glucose and its conversion to ethanol and carbon dioxide. Thirdly, the yeast respires – another aerobic reaction that happens when oxygen is available.

In the production of beer, brewers will always use their own special formula of yeast. The type of yeast used will not only affect the yield of alcohol, but it can also control the rate and intensity of fermentation, and ultimately the complex flavours that are created. Up until quite recently, distillers believed that yeast was only significantly involved with conversion rate and resilience. Yes, it must be able to convert a sugar-rich liquid containing zero alcohol up to perhaps 8% or more, and it needs to do it quickly. However, a few distilleries are starting to look a lot more closely at their yeast strain, since it's the yeast that builds the palate of flavours that the distiller has to play with. One such distillery is the London Distilling Company, which only became licensed in 2013, but it is taking its time trialling a few different yeast strains before gambling the life of the distillery on it! The Ben Nevis Distillery in Scotland is one of the only malt producers that uses a traditional brewer's yeast rather than hard-working distillery cultures. Meanwhile, in Wales, the Penderyn Distillery actually buys its beer in from the local Brains Brewery, a luxury not afforded to Scottish distilleries, which must by law mash and ferment on site. Yeast can be added to the fermenting vessel in one of two ways, either by literally tipping 20kg/44lbs. bags of living culture in by hand, or by pumping liquid yeast in through pipes. Malt whisky requires about 20kg/44 lbs. of (dry weight) yeast per ton of barley, or roughly 5g/⅙ oz. per litre/quart of wort.

Once the yeast and wort come into contact there's a period called the 'lag', which can last between three and six hours. Here, the yeast is acclimatizing itself to its new surroundings and preparing for the challenges ahead. The next stage is the 'log', where the yeast kicks into action. Deprived of the oxygen it needs to sustain itself, it begins to ferment the wort, producing ethanol, carbon dioxide and heat, at a serious pace, and multiplies in number rapidly. Most

RIGHT It's not always pretty (or perhaps it is), but fermentation arguably defines many of the parameters of flavour in whisky later down the line.

Fermentation tends to be around 3–4 days and the beer strength slightly higher than that of malt whisky, but this is partly due to corn having a higher percentage of fermentable sugars. In North America it is sometimes necessary to stop the wash/beer from getting too hot (which would endanger the yeast cells); many American fermenters feature cold water pipes to help to control this.

Generally, the time it takes to convert the sugar will depend on the temperature of the fermentation. The optimum temperature for any distillery depends on the specific strain of yeast, the sugar content of the wort and the desired outcome in terms of flavour – but typically you're talking about a starting temperature of around 20°C/68°F and an end temperature just above 30°C/86°F. In Scotland, there's usually little in the way of temperature control, other than lowering or increasing the starting temperature to counteract the seasons. This, in my opinion, is the first major turning point in the production process that can differentiate one distillery's character from another.

Even in longer fermentations, most of the alcohol is created in the first two days, but bacterial effects, which go on at the latter parts of the fermentation process, can help to develop wild, fruity and floral flavours that will carry through to the distillation stages. Fermentation produces many other things besides ethanol, including various other alcohols, aldehydes, acids and ketones. These are the building blocks of the final liquid's flavour profile and many of these also develop (in addition to the bacteria) in the later stages. The downside of dragging it out too long, though, is that some of the shiny new alcohol that has been created in the wash is wasted through oxidization – in other words, long fermentations make interesting flavour, but ultimately lose the distillery money.

washbacks are equipped with 'switchers', metal paddles that rotate around and suppress the foam that is generated. The fermentation of malt whisky usually begins to slow after 36 hours and most distilleries stop altogether at around 48–60 hours.

For malt whisky and North American whisky production the fermentation vessels are traditionally constructed of wood, but these days it's becoming more common to see steel ones, too. Glenrothes Distillery has 10 Oregon pine washbacks and eight steel. I have not personally tasted the beer produced from each side-by-side, but John MacLellan, distillery manager of Kilchoman on Islay, tells me that the difference is almost imperceptible. The most common wooden washbacks are made from Oregon pine, but you will also see Douglas fir (also a type of pine) and larch. American whisky fermenters can be made from steel, or wood, such as the Cypress wood vats at Four Roses Distillery. Bourbon distilleries often have a larger steel vat called a beer well, which is constantly topped up from the fermenters and used to supply a steady feed to the continuous stills.

In bourbon and rye whiskey production, the wort is not filtered after mashing; everything gets piped through to the fermenter and the solids are only removed later, during distillation.

⫸ SOUR MASH ⫷

Sour-mashing, sometimes known as 'set-back', is a process used in the production of many American whiskies. It is often mistaken as a proprietary technique of the Jack Daniel's brand, but, in fact, almost all of the bourbon producers in America conduct sour-mashing. It works in much the same way as sourdough bread, in that a portion of old mash (previously fermented beer) is added to fresh mash that is ready for fermentation. The old mash is actually taken from the leftovers of distillation, where the spent cereal solids are removed and drained of their sour liquid. The sourness is a result of lactic bacteria growth that occurs between fermentation and distillation. All the yeast is dead at this point. Then, the bacteria are killed by heating the liquid to 100°C/212°F. The liquid is next 'inoculated' with yeast (i.e. yeast is introduced to the liquid) before it is finally added into the new mash. It's believed by many that sour-mashing is an important stage of lowering the pH of the mash, which promotes good fermentation.

Traditionally, it probably worked slightly differently, wherein a repeat visit from the yeast culture of the last fermentation batch is thought to go some way towards ensuring consistency between batches. Set-back like this would have been the only method of inoculating the next batch of mash with yeast culture, rather than using a new culture every single time.

The sour part of the mash can make up over 20% of the fermented liquid, and the quantity used is strictly controlled to create a desirable pH for the yeast culture.

BELOW The contrast between old wooden walls and the palpable tension of of billions of yeast cells hard at work.

DISTILLATION

The art of distillation is certainly one of the more magical and esoteric parts of the whisky-making process. A juxtaposition between ancient copper kettles, the whirring of modern pumps and the steady flow of crystal-clear distillate lends a 'steampunk' feel to most distillery operations. It's fascinating to see that, despite technical advances, the alchemy of distillation has required the same amount of time and attention to detail for over 1,000 years. Even though some copper-pot distilleries now output annual bottle volumes in the tens of millions, the vast majority of distilleries in the world still use hand-made copper stills to produce their whisky, and many of them still check the strength of their spirit by floating a simple glass hydrometer.

THE FUNDAMENTALS OF DISTILLATION

Distillation does not make alcohol, but rather it concentrates it by removing many of the non-alcoholic components from an alcoholic wash. The reason that distillation works (and hence is the basis for the manufacture of all kinds of spirit) is that alcohol boils at 78.3°C (173°F), unlike water, which boils at 100°C (212°F), so the alcohol transforms into vapour before the water begins to evaporate. By heating the alcoholic wash to a very precise temperature, the alcohol vapours can be stripped out of the liquid, then cooled down and condensed into something stronger than what you started with. If the temperature is too hot, the vapour will contain too much water. If it's too cool, not enough vapour will make it through to the condenser.

So in principle, whisky distillation is quite simple – extracting ethanol out of a low-alcohol beer. Of course, the difficulty (and the exciting bit) comes with deciding which other bits, besides the alcohol, you want to take with you. Distillation is critical as it both *selects* and *creates* flavour. True, the fermentation process did a great job of that by itself, but the complex reactions don't stop there. In distillation our low-alcohol wash is finally exposed to high temperatures and phase changing – whether it be through steam coils, direct steam or direct heat. This prompts the further development of esters, aldehydes and other compounds related to oxidization.

There are a number of factors that dictate the strength of the stuff that comes out of the other end, and seemingly minor distinctions between distillation practices can have big repercussions in both the taste of the 'new-make spirit' (the final product of distillation) and the matured whisky. As we have already learned, fermentation creates numerous flavourful compounds, some of which the distiller will deem fit for the product and others that he or she won't.

LEFT A casual glance inside a pot still can only hint at the true alchemy that is taking place down below and up above.

RIGHT Three of the six 'onion'-shaped stills look out over sweeping countryside at the Royal Brackla distillery.

HOW WHISKY IS MADE

THE POT STILL

Of the two types of still used to distil whisky, the first is the traditional pot still and condenser used in the production of malt whisky and Irish pot-still whiskey. The pot still is always constructed entirely from copper on account of its high thermal conductivity, malleability and catalytic properties. The still normally looks like a giant teardrop-shaped kettle with a hatch for gaining access to the bottom and a pipe, called a lyne arm, that connects the top to a condenser. The contents of the still are heated by either a steam coil, pan or a direct flame; the alcohol vapours are stripped away from the liquid in the base, then the vapours bend around the top of the still (known as a swan neck) and fall down into the condenser to be turned back into liquid form.

You would think that holding a steady 78.3°C (173°F) during the course of the run would lead to a resulting distillate comprising pure alcohol, but of course water, while not boiling at this temperature, does still produce steam. It's for this reason that no matter what you do with a pot still, you'll never get close to producing pure 100% alcohol. Irish pot-still whiskey and Scottish malt whisky producers go some way towards overcoming this through batch distillation (re-distilling the distillate), thereby increasing the alcoholic strength of the liquid with each subsequent distillation.

The first distillation for malt whisky and Irish pot-still whiskey is conducted in a wash still, where 99% of the alcohol is extracted from the beer. Even with that careful control, the resulting liquid is unlikely to be above 25% alcohol by volume (ABV) and usually around 21–22%. This is not strong enough to make whisky, so the process is repeated once more for malt whisky (there are a handful of examples of more than two distillations) and twice more for Irish pot-

LEFT Bulbous and heavy-looking, the stills at Lagavulin are a defining part of the character of the final spirit.

still whiskey. After a second or third distillation, you can expect an alcohol strength of 65–85%.

STILL SHAPE AND SIZE

The shape, size and height of the still play a part in the final product. Most of it comes down to the phenomenon of reflux (the act of alcohol vapour returning to the still for further distillation). The higher the still, the greater the range of temperature from the top of the 'swan's neck' to the base of the pan. As vapour travels up a long still, it is more likely to lose momentum from the cooler copper at the top than it would in a stocky still (like the ones at Lagavulin), which retains most of its heat throughout. For the tall still, this means that only the lightest alcohols and the most volatile can make it 'over the top' and into the condenser. In squat little stills, the heavier, oilier and more dense flavour compounds are able to make it over the top since they have less distance to cover.

In addition to this, tall stills give a spirit more interaction time (and space) with copper. Copper has a purifying effect on a distilled spirit and a greater degree of interaction removes sulphurous flavours and heightens delicate fruit and floral aromatics. This is especially so in small stills, since there is a greater surface area of copper in comparison to the volume of liquid. Of course, the effects of size vary based on how much liquid is put into the still, too.

The shape of the still also has a part to play, with the different forms encouraging a varying degree of reflux in the system. A short still can produce spirit that is reminiscent of a tall still by bulging out and pinching in at certain stages up the neck of the still. Broadly, pot stills come in three traditional flavours: lantern-shaped, onion-shaped, and boil-ball (or boil-collar) shaped. Each of the different shapes is engineered to manipulate the amount of reflux that goes on during distillation by giving the vapours a clear run, or teasing them into crevices and overhangs that lead back down to the bottom.

Dalmore Distillery in the northern Highlands goes a step further by having a water-cooled jacket halfway up the neck of the still. This further lowers the temperature of the copper in that part of the still, generating exceptional amounts of reflux and a more delicate spirit. In a similar vein to this, a handful of distilleries use a purifier system, which comprises a pipe that runs from the beginning of the condenser down to the base of the still. What the purifier does is to capture any heavy, more oily volatiles that have *already* condensed back into liquid, while the lighter volatiles float on past and into the condenser proper – destined to become liquid a little further down the line. I have yet to see a still that has water mist sprayed directly onto it, which would seem to me to be a cheap and easy-to-control measure for dictating the level of reflux inside.

The final important factor in the shape of the still is the angle of the lyne arm. Some lyne arms angle upwards (Laphroaig, for example) and they will – just like a tall still – encourage reflux, as the design is effectively extending the length of vertical copper in the apparatus. Most lyne arms run perpendicular to the neck of the still, and a few slope steeply downwards. A downward-sloping lyne arm acts as a grabbing arm for vapour that makes it up to the top of the still's neck – snatching it into the condenser before it has a chance to drop.

It's not uncommon for distillers to become fixated over the condition of their still when it can be relied upon to turn out a good product. For example, I've heard reports of dents being deliberately hammered into new copper to replicate the condition of the metal it's replacing.

FIRING THE STILL

Just like skinning a cat, there's more than one way to heat a pot still. The traditional manner is with an open flame, which, aside from sounding quite dangerous, has a different effect on the liquid inside when compared with an indirect heat source (more on that shortly). The alchemist Paracelsus is credited with building the first water-jacketed still, way back in 1526. This gentler approach effectively made water the 'middle man' between the direct heat source and the fragile contents of the still, which gave greater temperature control and a decreased risk of burning. These days, pot stills are heated either by direct fire or through a steam coil. The coil is the more modern of the two methods and works the same way as an electric kettle – only it is steam that heats it rather than an electrical current. Coils are easy to control and produce a consistent diffusion of heat. Scapa Distillery on Orkney is thought to have been the earliest adopter of steam-powered stills, way back in 1885 when the distillery was founded.

Direct-fired stills are heated by either oil, gas, coal or (traditionally) peat fires. In the old days, this was quite a labour-intensive job – the fires would need to be constantly monitored, stoked, raked and sometimes even hosed down to control the temperature, lest the contents boil over into the condenser. Nowadays, there are only half-a-dozen distilleries in Scotland that use direct-fired stills and all are powered by gas or coal, with the exception of Springbank, which uses a combination of oil-firing and steam coils on its wash still. There still remain a few headaches with direct firing, namely the tendency for hotspots inside the still to scald and char the liquid at the still's surface. This is far more of a problem with the wash still, since a lot more insoluble free-flowing organic matter

clumps and sticks to the copper. The solution is the aptly named rummager: a long copper chain that mechanically swirls around the base of the still like a giant metal whisk.

So why all this fuss over how the damn thing is heated? You may well assume that heat is heat and that it has little bearing on the final product, but distillers are in agreement that direct firing produces a much 'heavier' spirit at the other end. In 1951, the Wine and Spirit Association of Great Britain mused that 'It is the unequal heating in parts (caused by direct firing) that develops the character and quality of Scotch whisky and brings out its special peculiarities.' It's for this reason that most distilleries resisted the transition to indirect firing right up until the 1960s.

Strathisla Distillery in Speyside is unique in having both direct-fired and indirect-fired stills; the produce of both stills are then blended to create their final product. Back in the days of dramming, the stillmen would always prefer to drink the 'cleric' (the spirit just as it comes out of the still, also known as 'white dog') from the direct-fired still. But on one occasion, the men were wrongly served cleric from the indirect-fired still and there was uproar among the workers, who immediately detected the difference.

Scientifically speaking, the most likely reason for heavier distillate character in direct-fired stills is the overheating of certain compounds in contact with the hot copper. In an indirect-fired still, the copper is heated by the liquid in the still (since the steam coil is not in contact with the copper), but with direct heat, it is the copper itself that diffuses the heat. This causes complex caramelizations, Maillard reactions (the chemical reactions

ABOVE The 16th century Swiss alchemist, Paracelsus, is credited with the invention of the first non-direct fired still.

between amino acids and carbohydrates that give browned foods their characteristic flavour) and charring of the solid matter in the wash still, which results in the breakdown and denaturing of various compounds in the wash and the production of furfural and sulphur compounds. These, in turn, will make their way into the alcohol vapour and impart a unique flavour into the spirit.

THE TWO TYPES OF CONDENSER

There are two types of condensers used in the production of pot-distilled whisky: the worm tub and the shell-and-tube.

The worm tub is based on a design that has been around for almost as long as distillation itself. From the end of the lyne arm, a pipe (usually copper) snakes down into a large, typically wooden tub filled with water. The longer and narrower the pipe, the better the cooling effect of the tub. At the bottom of the tub, the pipe exits and from there, the distillate runs out in liquid form. Worm tubs are normally open-topped and located outside the distillery walls, so that the famous Scottish weather can give a regular top-up. This is not without its pitfalls however, and the temperature of the cooling water can fluctuate by up to 20°C (68°F) from winter to summer. I'm reliably told that to counteract this, stills are run slightly slower in the summer. It's also their exposure to the elements that means regular cleaning is required to prevent the build-up of silt and debris. Before the introduction of shell-and-tube condensers, the worm tub was the only option. At the time of writing, there are 14 malt distilleries in Scotland that still use a worm tub. They insist that it produces a slightly richer and meatier spirit; I agree with them.

Shell-and-tube condensers rather fittingly consist of a cylindrical 'shell' with copper tubes running through it. They work the opposite way to a worm tub, whereby the tubes have cooling water running through them and the vapour condenses on the outside of the tubes,

TOP The very small and very unusual alembic-style still at Strathearn Distillery is controlled completely by hand and monitored by temperature gauges on the lyne arm and condenser.

ABOVE In contrast to Strathearn Distillery, the towering continuous still at Four Roses Distillery, Lawrenceburg, is a powerful indicator of the volume of product that your average Kentucky distillery outputs.

then rolls down to the bottom of the shell. What this means is that there is a greater surface area of copper for the vapour to cling to. This increased interaction between the copper and the vapour leads to a perceivably softer spirit. The shell-and-tube system is, in effect, a heat exchanger, and some distilleries now use the warmed-up cooling water to assist in the heating in other areas of the distillery. The super-modern Roseisle (or the 'Death Star' distillery as I have dubbed it) is one such site to do this – they recycle a massive 56% of all the energy expended there.

SPIRIT SAFE

The spirit safe can be found in every Scottish malt whisky distillery. It's a big brass and glass contraption with a heavy padlock on it and usually a steady flow of clear distillate running through it. The spirit safe was first trialled at Port Ellen Distillery on Islay in 1823, to coincide with the introduction of new excise duties, and was then quickly installed in all distilleries. The measure was put in place to address two conflicting issues – firstly that the distiller needed to have access to the spirit to determine when the necessary cuts and collections are made; and secondly, that the distiller was liable to steal the spirit or siphon it off to avoid payment of duties.

So what the spirit safe does, through a set of levers, is grant the stillman remote access to the flow of liquid without direct access to the liquid itself. The liquid's temperature and strength can be measured using the instruments locked inside the safe, and its capture can be modified by twisting the levers on the outside of the safe. Watching it always reminds me of someone manipulating radioactive material using rubber gloves attached to a sealed glass box. These days the world is a slightly more trusting place, however, and the distiller does actually have access to the inside of the safe, but up until 1983 only the local Customs and Excise officer, who often lived at the distillery, had the key.

ABOVE The spirit safe is a reminder in Scottish distilleries of the struggle between distiller and gauger in days gone by.

One distillery manager (who wishes to remain nameless) told me that once, when a thermometer inside the safe blew, he had to knock on the door of the excise officer's house to obtain the key to get inside. The thermometer was quickly replaced that day, but for a full week the distillery workers were, with expressions of sincerity on their faces, knocking on the Excise officer's door to borrow the key once more.

WASH DISTILLATION

In the first stage of distillation, the wash still is first filled about three-quarters full with preheated wort. From a 5–10% ABV wort, a distiller would expect to collect a 21–27% 'low wine' (the product of the first distillation) after a 5–8 hour distillation run. Typically, about one-third of the volume of the starting liquid will end up in low wines receiver. It's usual for the wash to froth and foam at the beginning of the distillation, which is something that can be monitored through the sight glass on the neck of the still. When this happens the heat is turned down to prevent boiling over.

Once all the low wines are collected, they're mixed with the 'foreshots' and 'feints' of the previous spirit distillation (see below). This is a curious practice that primarily aims to maintain consistency between runs and secondly to extract any additional ethyl-alcohol that may be lurking between folds of the feints.

SPIRIT DISTILLATION

The second (and in some cases, third) distillation concentrates the low wines from the first distillation and hones in the character particular to the distillery. Spirit stills are often, but not always, smaller than wash stills, since they usually have much less liquid to contend with.

Unlike the first distillation, which was allowed to go about its merry way, the second distillation must be carefully monitored by the stillman so that the correct strength, quality and volume of spirit is collected. The first trickles of liquid that come through the spirit safe are known as foreshots, which are channelled from the spirit safe to the feints receiver to be re-distilled. Foreshots are made up of hard-hitting compounds such as acetone (you may recognize this as the active ingredient in nail polish remover), acetaldehyde (ethereal and fruity) and methanol (ethanol's evil sister), as well as various intensely fruity esters (essentially pleasant-smelling chemicals formed when alcohol and an organic acid are mixed). Small amounts of these

chemicals can be desirable in the finished product, so it's up to the stillman to determine where the 'cut' is made (i.e. deciding which part of the distillate is collected for casking). It usually takes 5–35 minutes for the foreshots to finish coming through. Once the good stuff announces itself, the flow of liquid is redirected to the spirits receiver for collection. In the old days, the spirit would be tested by adding a splash of water; if it turned cloudy it meant that the high alcohols and acetone were still coming through. Clear meant it was safe to collect.

Exactly when the spirit collection is stopped is the choice of the distiller and a decision to be made based on the desired outcome of the product. Get too greedy and you'll be punished with a lower-strength spirit with very heavy, buttery, diesel and solvent-like aromas (these last parts of the run are known as 'feints'). Keep the collection to a minimum and the spirit will be stronger and taste lighter and more delicate... but you'll have a lot less of it.

The foreshots and feints are then ready to be mixed with low wines for the next spirit run. Now, those of you paying attention here may have noticed a slight mathematical issue with this. If the

BELOW The wash still and spirit stills at Glen Garioch Distillery, one of the oldest distilleries in the world.

foreshots and feints from every spirit run are mixed in with the low wines for the next, surely there would be a concentration of colourful compounds building up in the feints receiver over time? Well, it turns out that this is true and it's the reason why many feints receivers are periodically stripped of the dangerously alluring alien sludge that accumulates on the walls. Recently, I was told by Russell Anderson of Highland Park that cricket-ball-sized lumps of oxidized copper also collect in the feints receiver. This was something I found quite fascinating, because the seemingly clear spirit is obviously transporting a significant amount of solid matter at either the beginning or the end of the run. The feints receiver is cleaned out completely every summer at Highland Park, and Russell told me that there were enough of these blue copper balls to fill a large bag.

THE CONTINUOUS STILL

The second type of still used to distil whisky is the continuous still, which as the name suggests, involves an ongoing, continuous process that doesn't require all the 'stop–clean–start' frustration of batch distillation. The continuous still is sometimes referred to as a column still, patent still, or Coffey still, but they are all essentially the same piece of equipment. A quick glance at a still like this and you can immediately tell that it's very far removed from the backyard pot stills of whisky's past. Continuous stills look more like something you would find in an oil refinery than the home of your favourite whisky and are certainly a less romantic option than the pot still. They can be used to make characterless vodka, grain whisky, and are used in the production of many North American spirits, too, but what they lack in small-batch grittiness, they

more than make up for in epic scale, efficiency and consistency.

The continuous still is usually made up of two towers. The first tower, known as the analyser, has a series of 'baffle plates' throughout its length, which are perforated sections that effectively each conduct their own mini distillation. Alcoholic wash is pumped into the top of the tower and allowed to flow down through apertures in the plates, while hot steam is pumped in at the bottom and rises as vapour. Where the two meet, the steam strips away the alcohol from the wash, causing it to rise up the column; as the steam and alcohol approach the top of the column, the heavier steam begins to lose pace and falls back down, mixed in with all the dregs of the watery wash. The strong alcohol exits the top of the column as vapour and is directed to the bottom of the next column, the rectifier. This part works like a condenser, but also does the job of separating the different alcohols. The spirit vapour rises up the column and is cooled by cold liquid running through the system. The molecules with the highest boiling point will condense first, and they are drawn off and mixed back in with the continuous flow of wash that enters the analyser. Further up the column, though, ethanol will begin to condense, and it's here that the column is tapped and the spirit extracted. Highly volatile molecules, with low boiling points, might make it all the way to the top, and they too will be mixed back in with the new wash for re-distillation.

RIGHT A peek inside a continuous still shows one of the many 'bubble plates' that lines the column. Each bubble forms a pathway between the plate below and the airspace above, granting passage only to the lighter (stronger) vapours.

HOW WHISKY IS MADE

As if all that weren't clever enough, the cool liquid that runs through the rectifier is actually new wash headed for the analyser. While it performs the task of cooling the alcohol vapour, the vapour warms it up, so little energy is wasted. The strength and purity of the resulting liquid is controlled by where on the column the alcohol is drawn off, as well as the temperature of the various parts of the system, and how hard (fast) the system is run.

Because the still doesn't need to stop (they are still cleaned and maintained intermittently) and requires very little in the way of human interaction, a column still also costs less to run. The downside, which can also be seen as an upside, is that the spirit that it produces is lighter and far less characterful. Continuous distillations tend to form fewer esters during the process, probably due to the slightly lower heat involved. They also tend to have fewer furfurals (caramel, burnt sugar flavours, fusel oils and floral qualities. This is in part due to precise selection of alcohol and in part to do with the stricter control of heat in the process. Having said that, a column still is capable of making a tasty whisky both in Scotland and in Irish and North American distilleries.

DISTILLATION IN NORTH AMERICA

Now that we've ascertained the difference between a column still and a pot still, allow me to introduce you to the most commonly used still in North America, which combines both of these methods in one.

In a typical bourbon distillery, the unfiltered beer (or 'wash') passes into a column still, where it is typically distilled to around 60–62% ABV. Then, the low wine goes on for a second distillation in what is essentially a pot still called a 'doubler', where it comes off at about 67% ABV. Try as I did, I couldn't find a good reason why the pot still is called a 'doubler' other than that it is the second part of a double distillation. Some people put it down to the doubler actually doubling the speed of distillation by taking some of the strain away from the column. Interestingly, the use of doublers is not actually required by law in the bourbon-making process.

There are two whiskey distilleries in North America (Early Times and Bernheim) that use a type of still called a 'thumper' instead of the doubler. The thumper works in much the same way, the only difference being that the spirit is still in vapour form when it enters the thumper. The noise generated by the expanding and contracting of the thumper is where it gets its name. This kind of set-up dates back to the days of moonshining, where the thumper would have been made out of a cask. Back then, the thumper or doubler would have contained liquid (often beer) which the distillate would bubble through, extracting additional alcohol in the process.

MATURATION

The maturation of whisky in the cask is undeniably the single biggest contributor of flavour in the whisky-making process. It's at this stage that the pungent distillery characteristics of new-make spirit are, over time spent encased in wood, transformed into a more mellow and relaxed liquid through a series of complex chemical changes. By my reckoning, even in young whisky with a sturdy distillery character, the cask is responsible for 50% of the flavour of the final product. This is especially true of first-fill (i.e. previously unused) American oak casks that are used in bourbon production, and perhaps less true in heavily peated Islay whiskies, where the phenolics that are derived from the kiln-drying process still hold a firm grip on the flavour profile of the dram. In very old whisky, I think it's fair to say that the lasting influence of wood can lay claim to over 90% of the whisky's flavour profile, where almost all the nuances of the earlier process have been drowned out.

The ageing of the product is also the last significant stage in the process, a fact that in itself makes maturation the most important bit. An ugly-duckling new-make spirit can still grow into a beautiful swan if nurtured correctly by a good nose and an exceptional cask. Likewise, a new-make spirit with all the potential in the world will be destined for paint thinner if ravaged by the negative effects of a defective cask.

The act of placing spirit in a cask and leaving it to do its thing may seem like a simple one, and when described like that, I suppose it is. But there is a whole range of variables that can impact the outcome, from the type of oak to the size of cask, toasting or charring, climate and temperature fluctuation, and of course, time. It's for this reason that all producers of whisky will have a 'wood policy' in place, designed not around a complete understanding of the process, since that does not exist, but through knowledge of past experiences and tradition.

HOW WHISKY IS MADE

The resting of whisky in cask almost certainly came about through the use of wood as means of transportation and storage, rather than gastronomic pursuit. Even though wine and beer had been held in casks since at least 500 BC, the French and Dutch were probably the first to notice the positive effects that time in wood had on their *brandewijn* (brandy) as it was shipped from Cognac up to the Netherlands, back in the 15th century. And it would appear that shipping spirits over long distances is the cause for many producing regions gaining notoriety for the quality of their product. For example, Mescal made in the town of Tequila in the 18th century was stretched and squeezed though hot days and cold nights on its journey to North America. Likewise, rum barrels were shipped from the Caribbean islands to the four corners of the world.

It's likely that casks were used in the production of Scotch malt whisky at least as far back as the 17th century, where English oak would have been used by coopers, but exactly when it became the norm is not entirely clear. One of the earliest references to the positive effects of whisky in cask comes from Elizabeth Grant's *Diary of a Highland Lady*, which was written around the turn of the 19th century. She describes a cask of Glenlivet whisky that was sent to King George III (the mad one). Ironically, Glenlivet was an illicit, non-tax- paying operation at the time of her writing. She writes of 'whisky, long in wood, long in uncorked bottles, mild as milk, and the true contraband gout in it'. Although casks were used for moving large quantities of whisky around Scotland, most of the whisky made there in the early 19th century was for local consumption. Most of the time, whisky had little need to be stored *en masse*, especially given the comparatively small production capacity of the numerous operations. Whisky production was seasonal back then, though, so it's fairly

likely that barrels were used to accumulate stock, but in most instances, the local population had no patience to wait for it, so they quite often simply ran out.

It would have been around the same time that the Americans, with their newly acquired independence, first noticed a marked improvement in the quality of their corn and rye whiskies. The landlocked states of Kentucky and Tennessee needed to move large quantities of liquor long distances to the higher-populated coastal regions. Weeks of travel by boat or over rough terrain softened the whiskey through agitation and time, improving its quality. Demand for this higher-quality whiskey increased. This is one of the benefits of having almost all of the veteran distilleries of North America situated a great distance inland – maturation was unavoidable, and with that came an improvement in whiskey character.

It wasn't until 1915, during the 'What is Whisky?' debate (see page 25), that it became compulsory for Scotch to be rested in oak barrels for a minimum of two years, extending to three years in 1916. During the early part of the 20th century, chestnut wood was as common a container as oak, and it wasn't until as late as 1990 that the British government passed an order declaring that only oak could be used. There are more than likely thousands of old chestnut casks in Scotland, which, if bottled and marketed as whisky, would actually be in breach of whisky's current legal definition!

From 1960 onwards, a change in legislation required bourbon to be aged only in new oak. This generated a sizeable surplus of perfectly good ex-bourbon casks, which were sold at rock-bottom prices to European whisky-makers. From then onwards, the use of ex-Sherry casks (which had previously been the norm) dropped off considerably. Even today, around 90% of Scotch is matured in bourbon wood and the remaining 10% in ex-Sherry and wine casks.

LEFT The maturation warehouse is perhaps the most exciting yet peaceful part of a distillery.

THIS PAGE Ricks of dried timber are trimmed by hand, so that they are narrower at each end; they are then passed on to the cooper who raises a single cask every two minutes.

CONSTRUCTING CASKS

There are two main families of oak used for ageing whisky: white oak (*Quercus alba* is the most common but there are many others), and red oak (only *Quercus robur* or *Quercus sessilis*). White oak comes from America, and red oak from Europe, but America imports around a quarter of the total European oak exports and Europe its fair share of American white oak. The trees themselves resemble their cultural counterparts in some ways, too. White oak has a paler-coloured bark than red oak, but there's little difference between the colour of the cut wood. Red oak grows slowly; it twists and turns and only reaches maturation after 150 years. The resulting whisky is a more tannic (a trait arising from the slow growth), peppery and spicy with, rather fittingly, flavours of red-coloured things like cherries, grapes and red apples. White oak grows much faster, and it grows straight and true because it's planted with more space, accelerating along to maturation in only 60–80 years. The result is a more 'obvious' wood influence, with plenty of vanilla and associated white-coloured things, like banana, white chocolate, buttermilk and custard.

From a visual examination of the wood alone, it's difficult to tell the difference between the two, but one way to distinguish them is by examining a cut cross-section of the wood. Both types of wood are porous along the growth lines of the wood, but the pores on the white oak are actually filled with tylose (a kind of natural wood-filler), whereas red oak pores are open. The tylose in the white oak actually makes the wood slightly more watertight than red oak. Sometimes it's easier to feel the difference with your fingers when looking for the pores, with red oak feeling a little less smooth than the white oak. Another way of telling the difference is by examining the medullary rays on the grain of the wood. These rays are small, dark pencil dashes that run with the grain of the wood, and on red oak they tend to be under 10mm/⅓ inch in length, while on white oak, they tend to be around 20mm/¾ inch in length. Since the medullary rays are considered to be completely impervious to liquids, it is yet another point in favour of white oak as the better container. White oak is also straighter and more malleable. Red oak, grown mostly in the forests of northern Spain and France, is naturally inferior at all of the same things and it takes longer to accomplish it. But red oak does have the advantage of being slightly longer-

THIS PAGE Head hoops, quarter hoops and bilge hoops are applied, then the barrel is tested for leaks.

lasting than white, and it is highly regarded by some for the flavour that it imparts in whisky.

Also becoming more common are the French oak (*Quercus petraea*), which is much-loved by the Cognac industry, and *Quercus mongolica*, an expensive oak revered by the Japanese and prized for its tropical fruit and heady incense aromatics.

After felling, the wood is first dried for up to a year, in log form. Next it is sliced into quarters, like batons of a carrot, then cut down to stave billets that follow the grain of the wood. Bourbon barrels are usually cut with a slightly curved saw that traces the curvature of the barrel along the width of the stave. European cuts are normally straight and the wood is later trimmed to form flush joints between staves. There's significant wastage from the tree, comprising bits of wood too small to be made into staves, but some coopers use the waste to fuel the fires used in the toasting or charring stages later.

Only the inner 80% of the log, known as the heartwood, is used since the outer sapwood, which sits directly behind the bark, is too porous. Most American oak staves that are destined for American whiskey maturation are traditionally kiln-dried for about 30 days at this stage. This takes its moisture level down from 50% to 12% and the wood is then ready to be

coopered into a cask. Oak used by the Sherry industry in Europe, on the other hand, is yard-dried in stages for a further nine months to three years; typically, this brings the moisture content down to around 14%. Some bourbon producers are now experimenting with yard-drying their wood in the pursuit of better flavour release; Woodford Reserve even released a 'Seasoned Oak-finished' expression that saw aged bourbon infused with five-year-dried oak.

What's the difference, you may ask? Well, if you'd asked 20 years ago, the answer may have been nothing. But kiln-drying is quite an aggressive process, and recent studies suggest that the kiln-dried wood skips an important stage of fungal growth that assists in the conversion and liberation of flavoursome compounds in the wood. By contrast, yard-dried wood plays host to a succession of travelling microscopic fungi during its seasoning period, which 'acupuncture' hydrogen peroxide into the surface of the wood, softening and relaxing the harder structure of the wood, and therefore allowing better penetration from the spirit. The fungi, along with rainfall, are also thought to assist in the removal of tannins, even leaving behind a visible

THIS PAGE The various components of a barrel's life, from preparation for dumping (far left) to the charring of its inner surfaces (above) and the cooper's tools (left).

tea-stain of tannin on the ground where the wood had been placed.

Staves are born straight, so to form the familiar barrel shape they must be trimmed down and bent into submission. The stave is cut so that it tapers in at either end – a necessary step to form the bulge in the barrel. The bulge is an essential feature that physically helps to hold the barrel together and aids in the manoeuvrability of the barrel by hand.

The bulge allows the barrel to be easily rocked and rolled about the place, despite weighing in excess of 400kg/880 lbs. A 180-litre/190-quart bourbon cask is constructed from roughly 30 finished staves, which are placed in hoops, then heated by steam and forced together mechanically. A 500-litre/528-quart cask (or 'butt') needs approximately 50 staves. They are formed in a similar way, but usually warmed with an open flame and water (to prevent cracking) before being bent into shape.

The circular barrel ends are made from shorter stave cuts that are drilled out and pinned together with dowel rods (solid, cylindrical pins used to fasten two staves together) to form a square. They are then sawn into a circle and sent on for toasting or charring along with the barrel shell.

Toasting and charring are not interchangeable terms, although they might sound the same. Charring is an all-out flamethrower assault on the interior surfaces of the barrel, as ruthless licks of heat blast the wood for up to 30 seconds, causing the surface to bubble and writhe as it catches fire. One legend describes how the charring process was introduced by the Reverend Elijah Craig (the dubiously proclaimed inventor of bourbon), who wanted to store his whiskey in oak casks that had previously held fish (other reports state that they formerly contained nails), so he aggressively charred the inside to remove the fishy flavour. Whether it was Craig or not, I'd say that there's a good chance that the man or woman who did first char a cask was intending to overcome a similar problem.

When a cask is toasted, the heat is applied more gently, sometimes through convection rather than direct flame, and over a longer period of time – up to and around six minutes. Toasting is kind of like roasting a sausage slowly, whereas charring is something akin to barbecuing a sausage quickly. Visually, there is a similar contrast, too. Charred barrels look as if they have (barely) survived a pirate-ship battle, with blackened scabs and brittle blisters. A light char is the colour of graphite and a heavy char is as black as coke. The colour of the internal surfaces of a toasted cask on the other hand can range from vanilla fudge through to dark coffee. The toast level is controlled during the process and categorized as either light, medium, medium+ or dark. The general rule of thumb is that barrels intended for the bourbon industry (which are always white oak) are charred, and barrels

intended for Sherry, Madeira, Port or other types of wine are toasted. The Brown-Forman Cooperage in Kentucky, which produces casks for Woodford Reserve and Jack Daniel's, among others, actually toasts its casks before charring, in a kind of why-do-one-when-you-can-do-both approach. The Independent Stave Company, which makes barrels for most of the rest of the American whiskey industry, offers a computer-controlled barrel-profiling service, where its customers can request specific flavours and the cask is charred to a unique heat curve – like roasting coffee to liberate a distinct aroma.

Whether by toasting or charring, the heat treatment of these casks is a critical step in the influence of flavour in whisky. Indeed, the impact that the cask's toast or char has over the final whisky cannot be overstated. Grilling the barrel like this achieves three functions – the degradation of wood polymers into flavoursome compounds, the destruction of unpleasant resinous compounds in the wood, and in the case of charring, the forming of a thin layer of active carbon. I would also propose that the char or toast assists in fusing the spirit to the wood by absorbing the liquid and holding it close to the adjacent wood surface – kind of like pressing a wet sponge against your skin.

In the final stage of production, the barrel ends are securely fitted and wax-sealed, then the bung hole is drilled. The container is then tested for leaks and filled with a splash of water to prevent it from drying out before filling. The process is now complete. Now the cask is a giant teabag in reverse; a potent package of densely clustered compounds, ready to reap slow, sapid domination on any liquid fortunate enough to be imprisoned within its walls.

PUTTING CASKS TO USE
In the production of American straight whiskey and bourbon, the liquid must be aged in charred new white oak barrels, which imparts a lot of colour and associated wood characteristics into the

spirit in a very short time. The combination of fresh wood and warm climate means that bourbon matures quickly. The minimum age required is two years and many products available are little more than four years old. The characteristics we associate with bourbon are largely derived from this wood policy.

Once bourbon casks have been used, they cannot be regenerated or re-used again for American whiskey (with the exception of corn whiskey – see page 104). It's not a problem, though, as there's plenty of demand for casks from tequila and rum producers, as well as other whisky producers around the world. The bourbon casks are either broken down into staves for shipment, or, as is often the case more recently, left in barrel form and sent off to their new homes. Irish, Canadian, Japanese and Scotch whisk(e)y producers all use ex-bourbon casks to age the majority of their whiskies, where it's common practice to cooper ex-bourbon casks (with capacities of 180 litres/190 quarts) into slightly larger hogshead casks (250 litres/264 quarts by slipping in a few extra staves.

You may wonder why the Scotch whisky industry would use American cast-offs. Why not build casks intended solely for malt whisky maturation? Well, the answer to this lies in the requirements of two styles of whisky. Two of my younger brothers used to share boiled eggs at breakfast-time. One of them liked the egg white, and the other the yolk. The first brother would peel the whites off and eat them, then he would pass the yolks on to the other brother. Bourbon barrels are the same deal. American whiskey producers demand the initial flavours of coconut ice cream, hard toffee and cream soda, which can only be provided by charred new American oak. Conveniently, these are the flavours that other whisky-makers wish to avoid. Essentially, the bourbon industry gets exactly what it wants from the cask before passing it on to the next guy, who can be confident that the cask has been sufficiently depleted of the bits he doesn't want.

And it's the same situation with the wine industry in Europe. While the flavours may be slightly different in the initial hit of a toasted oak cask, the extraction of them into Sherry and other wines remains an important step towards a cask that is fitting for malt whisky maturation.

So the first liquid to enter a new cask knocks out the high notes of the wood, but what of the liquid's impression on the cask? Can you detect whether an oak cask previously held Sherry or Madeira? A typical Sherry butt is thought to 'in-drink' somewhere around 10 litres/ 10.5 quarts of sherry over a two-year period, but many casks have water added to them in the interim period to draw out the wine – so the question is whether you might be able to detect a few litres of Sherry added to 500 litres/528 quarts of whisky. This is a matter that is open to debate, and I know of some who claim that it is impossible to detect the difference between different wines that the cask held in previous fills, yet many producers place great emphasis on the past affairs of their wooden barrels. I personally think that the effect of the previous fill is increased over time; having tried some very old (50+ years) Sherry-cask single malts, I can certainly testify to considerable (to the point of incredible) Sherry influence. Perhaps, like many of us, it just takes a while for past relationships to eke out of the system.

This leads us on to the topic of finishing, whereby a whisky that is considered to be aged sufficiently is 'finished' in a cask of a different type in an efforts to imbue the spirit with further complexity and character. This is a much more common practice in malt whisky, but there are some examples of bourbons, such as the Angel's Envy, that spend a short time in ruby Port casks, and Maker's 46, which has (new) French oak staves introduced during its maturation.

In the case of finishing in malt whisky, there are examples of Port, Madeira, oloroso, fino, Pedro Ximénez (PX), Bordeaux, Burgundy, Muscat and many

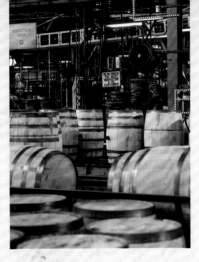

other types of casks used in finishing whisky today. The question is, though, how apparent is the flavour of the previous inhabitant when finishing is typically only six to 24 months? Not much, in my opinion. Sure, if your whisky squats in a PX cask for a couple of years, with all its sultana/golden raisin and black cherry sweetness, there will be some noticeable influence; Lagavulin Distillers Edition is a great example of this – but to differentiate between different sherries and wines, I think is a stretch.

Interestingly, there are no official rules around the use of the term 'Sherry cask' in Scotch whisky production. This means that the cask could be a cheaper, ex-bourbon cask, that has had only the most fleeting of brief encounters with Sherry, or a new cask that has only been briefly seasoned with Sherry. The neglect to tackle this point has left the door open for producers to 'rejuvenate' dead or drying casks by seasoning them with Paxarete, a type of very sweet wine. A small quantity of the concentrated wine is added to a cask, and the vessel is sealed and pressurized, causing the wine to percolate into the wood. Any excess wine is drained from the barrel and is then sent off for filling with whisky. I should say that this practice is thought to be far less common today, but it strikes me as odd that even though it's illegal to adulterate Scotch whisky with flavourings, it's not illegal to adjust the flavouring of the vessels that it is stored in.

TIME AND TEMPERATURE

Time is the most obvious variable in the maturation process. We're all familiar with gauging maturation characteristics by looking for a number on a bottle, and all-too-often placing our faith in it as a marker of quality. Sadly, the maturation process is not as simple as 'the longer you leave it, the more woody it gets', and certainly not as simple as the older the

whisky, the better it tastes. An age statement can be useful, but only really becomes relevant if the other variables are made aware to us. And even today that scarcely happens. Without information like the type of cask and its condition, char/toast level and warehouse conditions, the age statement becomes an arbitrary figure and you're better-off assessing the whisky on the quality of the box it comes in and the size of the distiller's shoes.

The best wood that money can buy will be no use if warehouse conditions are not taken into account. Temperature and humidity of the maturation environment both play critical roles in the rate of ageing as well as the inevitable loss of product through evaporation.

The size of the cask also has a bearing on maturation speed. Larger casks have a higher surface-area-to-volume ratio, meaning that there are fewer square centimetres/inches of wood per millilitre/fluid ounce of liquid. Small casks have a lower surface-area-to-volume ratio, meaning that there's more wood to go around per millilitre/fluid ounce of spirit. You might think that this means faster ageing for smaller casks, and to an extent this is true. Wood extractives are found in higher concentrations in smaller casks, but there's no substitute for time. Because some of the job is done much quicker in small casks, there is a risk of too much wood character being imparted, so the whisky is removed. The flip side to this, though, is that other important oxidative and ester-creating reactions that can take longer have had too little time to make an impact. The result? In my experience, small casks impart a kind of pseudo-maturation; while many of the familiar markers are there, it somehow seems rushed and immature. You can dress a baby in a man's clothes, but underneath the bow tie and sharp suit, it's still a baby.

And then there's the alcoholic strength of the liquid in the cask to consider. Most of the Scotch whisky industry fills its casks at 63.5% ABV which, through trial and error over the years, has been deemed the optimum mix for a neat and even extraction from the cask. Within the realms of sensible fill strengths, the following rules generally apply: lower-strength (more watery) liquids extract more tannin and sugar, whereas higher strength spirits extract more lactones (think coconut and butter) and, rather surprisingly, less colour, but also make more sugars available by breaking down hemicellulose and lignin. Tests show that raising the fill strength from 55%–75% ABV can cut sugar levels by half over typical maturation periods.

Some malt whisky distilleries do fill higher than 63.5% ABV, with one obvious benefit being that fewer casks are required. Scotch grain whisky is

commonly put to cask at 67–68% ABV. Irish whiskey is commonly filled at 71% ABV, but there are no legal limits regulating it. In America, whiskeys that are destined to be sold as 'straight' or as bourbon cannot enter the cask at over 62.5% ABV, and from what I can tell, most producers fill at the legal limit. Canadian whisky usually sits between 68–72% ABV, but can be anywhere up to 78% ABV, as per Hiram Walker.

Local climate has always been a contributing factor in how a whisky tastes and feels. Cold, wet winters and mild, humid summers in Scotland slow things down to a snail's pace, whereas the racked warehouses in Kentucky can reach in excess of 60°C (140°F) in the dry summer heat. Japan's first whisky distillery, Yamazaki, was located in the misty hills around Kyoto on account of its climatic similarity to the Scottish Highlands.

Warehouses come in two types: traditional dunnage warehouses, where casks are laid on a floor in rows, called stows, stacked two, three or four levels high; and the more modern equivalent (popular in the US), of a racked warehouse, where floor-to-ceiling shelves hold the casks. Aesthetically, the dunnage warehouses are more pleasing, because there's a timeless feel about them, but there are other things at work here besides looking pretty. In a tall, racked warehouse the temperature can vary by as much as 40°C (104°F) from the bottom to the top. This means that casks at the top will mature in a different way to those at the bottom, an effect that is combatted by a constant rotation of stock.

This brings into question the matter of humidity. Some loss of liquid (the 'angel's share') is inevitable when maturing spirits. In Scotland, Ireland and Japan, this tends to be around 2% of the liquid in the barrel every year, the larger proportion of which is alcohol. In hotter climates like Kentucky and Tennessee, it can be up to 5%, but it depends on the position and temperature of the warehouse. Big brands have gone to great lengths to reduce the angel's share, since it is effectively their profits that are disappearing into the ether. One large corporation even conducted trials of cling-filmed/plastic-wrapped casks, but the experiment failed. Two-way interaction between the barrel and the world outside is essential; the angel's share is the lesser of two evils.

In high-humidity environments, the ethanol (alcohol) depletes at a quicker pace than the water, meaning that the ABV of the liquid lowers over time – this is the way of things in Scotland. In very dry conditions, the water will evaporate faster than the alcohol, as is often the case in Kentucky, especially near the roof of a racked warehouse. This explains why some cask-strength bourbons are often many degrees higher than permissible.

THE IMPACT OF OAK

Much of what goes on in the perpetual twilight of a warehouse is unpredictable without the analysis of every stave of wood that makes up every cask and every drop of liquid that goes into it. The impracticality of this is obvious, so a whisky 'nose' relies on experience, senses and, of course a little science to gauge the quality of a cask and the optimum time that a whisky should spend in it. Besides systematic testing and tasting, the ageing process is most often a simple guarding of treasure that has yet to achieve its full

worth. The changes that take effect in the murky realms of the vessel are even today being scrutinized and tested to better understand the effects of the barrel and the optimum maturation conditions for the whisky. Below I've given a pitifully brief explanation of the goings-on inside a cask. Having said that, it's likely that you will encounter some unfamiliar words and terms, so wherever possible I have tried to relate them to the ultimate reason for all of this: flavour.

Oak itself contains over 100 volatile opponents capable of contributing flavour in a whisky. Additionally, there are other compounds formed through the oxidation of wood extracts and compounds already present in the new-make spirit. Finally, there are certain subtractive effects caused by the char layer of a bourbon cask. Think of maturation like building a house brick-by-brick, the only difference being that your bricks can appear and morph in size at will, walls are prone to disappear in their entirety, and you have virtually no control over the shapes and sizes of the rooms!

The additive effects of the wood come from four potential sources that make up much of the composition of oak: lignin, hemicellulose, extractives, and oak tannins.

Lignin makes up around 25% of the oak, and it's this stuff that provides much of the aromatic qualities of woodsmoke, as well as some very important acids, phenols and aldehydes that influence whisky flavour. One example of a compound, derived from the heating of lignin during toasting or charring, is guaiacol, an aromatic oil that contributes roasted qualities reminiscent of coffee or toast to the liquid. Guaiacol is also a precursor to other flavourful compounds, like vanillin, which gives us caramel, chocolate, toffee, cream and vanilla aromatics; and eugenol (see page 92). Lignin is broken down more or less linearly as maturation continues, so expect these flavours to increase over time.

Hemicellulose is the breeze block of oak's secondary cell walls, and is thought to react with complex acids in the spirit, causing the extraction of simple wood sugars (around 200 different types) that provide body and smoothness to the liquid. The treatment of the wood during coopering causes some of these sugars will undergo caramelization, too. The sugars provide little in the way of actual sweetness, but they are thought to knock back some undesirables, and the caramelized sugars can give plenty of associated aromatic sweetness. This includes compounds like furfural (an aldehyde formed from the sugar xylose), which has a nutty aroma, and cyclotene, with its distinctive maple syrup and liquorice/licorice flavours.

Extractives are free-running compounds that are 'washed' out of the wood. Important extractives include eugenol, which encompasses a whole family of dry, spicy flavours like nutmeg and cinnamon. Also attending the party are oak lactones (coconut aroma); then there's a whole range of other unpronounceables that give us subtle, grassy, baked, wood-sap, peachy, floral and even greasy aromas.

Wood tannin gives the familiar drying sensation on the palate, and when managed correctly, it adds balance and grip to an otherwise flabby spirit. Tannins also help to combat a sulphury character in young whiskies, and act as a crude marker of overall wood influence by stabilizing colour. Tannins, although odourless, are also catalysts for oxidative reactions, so they do indirectly affect whisky aroma. It's thought that differences in the levels of tannins and extractives between white oak and red oak is the main defining factor in the character of the whisky that they each produce.

In addition to the additive effects of the wood, the charred layer of carbon on the inside of the bourbon cask adds a different slant to the process when compared to the toasted European cask. It's thought that the thin layer of active carbon acts as a kind of filtration system by locking down undesirable compounds that may be present in the whisky, like dimethyl sulphide (DMS), which asserts a cabbage-like aroma on white dog and new-make whisky. In effect, this carbonic layer further accelerates the maturation process by stripping distillery character, while the cask goes to work on adding new stuff.

Finally, there is colour, on which I think too much emphasis is placed. Although colour plays an important part in flavour perception, bending our better judgement towards grass, fresh fruit and heather when a whisky has a green tinge, and plums, florals and jam when the whisky is red – it is in truth little more than an indicator of cask type and condition. I have tasted 40-year-old malt whiskies with only a soft straw colour, and I have tasted three-year-old bourbons the colour of orange Fanta. Likewise, I have a 1981 bottle of Karuizawa on my shelf that is the colour of molasses. Perhaps some approximate forecasting can be made of a whisky's flavour-profile based on the assessment of colour alone (dark hues are sometimes an indication of tannin), but how much of this is our mind's curious ability to make red things taste 'red', I do not know. It's far better to drink it than to look at it, in this author's opinion.

Extraction of colour is for the most part a linear process – the longer the time in cask, the darker the colour gets. The exception to this is the first 6–12 months of ageing, especially in new-oak casks, (particularly applicable to the American whiskey industry). During the early stages of maturation, the spirit will take on an increased initial splash of gold, as free extractives invade the liquor. Once these 'easy-pickings' compounds are exhausted it's back to the usual breakdown of lignin and other colour-contributing wood components over time.

Last, but certainly not least, is the chemical degradation of the liquid through oxidation. Besides ethanol, there are numerous other trace alcohols present in the spirit. Each alcohol has its own style and is subject to the effects of oxidation, resulting in the formation of a aldehydes and acids. For example, the oxidation of the ethanol (alcohol) in the cask forms acetaldehyde and acetic acid. Aldehydes play an important role in whisky aroma, like benzaldehyde (created through the oxidation of benzyl alcohol), which smells like almond.

Acetic acid, along with other oxoacids, is crucial for the formation of esters. Esterification is where an acid reacts with an alcohol and creates a new, highly aromatic compound. Isoamyl acetate, which provides the banana aroma that is prevalent in Jack Daniel's, is formed when isoamyl alcohol reacts with acetic acid. Esters provide all of the fruity and floral top notes in whisky aroma, everything from geranium or jasmine right through to apple, sage, pineapple and strawberry.

REFILLING AND REJUVENATING

Just because a cask has been (re)filled once, it doesn't mean it's straight to the knacker's yard to be turned into a plant pot. At the time of writing, a new bourbon cask costs about £250/$420 and gets sold on after its first fill for around £150/$250. An ex-Sherry butt costs about £700/$1,175. For non-bourbon producers, the cost works out to be just over £1/$1.7 per litre/quart of whisky that the cask will hold, which makes wood the most expensive raw ingredient (and it is an ingredient) in the bottle. The canny Scotsman always has an eye on his wallet, so it should come as no surprise that it's common practice to refill casks, sometimes two or three times, in an effort to get your money's worth.

Refilling is not as simple a practice as it may sound, though, because, as previously mentioned, the cask will not necessarily continue in the same manner that it started. All of the contributing compounds in oak play a part, but some are exhausted in a matter of weeks, and for others it may take decades. Some readily soluble compounds will diminish after the first fill and others will continue to influence on subsequent fills; like reusing coffee grounds, the effect is not only a lighter influence but disparity in balance, too.

ABOVE Most coopers have to repair their own tools these days, because it's very difficult to buy new ones!

At some point, however, the towel has to be thrown in. Once a cask becomes 'inactive', efforts to extract anything worthwhile will be mostly fruitless, and what was once a bundle of flavour potential becomes a vapid husk. Casks like this are sometimes used for vatting together malt whisky before bottling. Failing that, there is always the option of rejuvenation. Rejuvenation is like sanding down a floor and reapplying the varnish. It involves mechanically scraping the inside of the cask to remove the char or toast, as well as the surface directly behind it, then re-charring or re-toasting the cask to bring it back to life again.

Blending is the art of combining whiskies of different ages, from different distilleries, with the aim of making a product of a specific style and price. Most blended whisky is a combination of grain whisky and malt whisky, but there are also blended (or vatted) malts available, which are literally a mixture of different malt whiskies. Blending achieves a number of different things but, more than anything, it offers whisky a more competitive price than the costly-to-produce single malts. Having said that, there are some very expensive blends out there, too, which is a subject that I will tackle a little later on.

Blends also traditionally offer a more consistent product, since in the past malts tended to be a little inconsistent. However, malt producers have done a good job at smoothing over bumps in the road in recent years, and I see little reason to avoid drinking a malt for fear of it not tallying with your memory of it. Finally, blends are balanced. For the same reason that we blend tea, coffee, fragrances, paint and spices, it allows us to take disjointed or unexceptional elements and combine them into something greater and perhaps unachievable were it not for the careful mixing of components.

I like to think of a blend like a piece of music, where the instruments represent the various sections of an orchestra. Some malt whiskies are best compared to light and delicate string instruments, and others are more like the brass or percussion section. The blender is the composer, selecting whiskies based on what they bring to the piece. The difficulty comes when re-creating that composition time and time again. In an orchestra you would find the best musicians of their time to play the piece, but as any concert-goer knows, there will always be subtle changes to the arrangement in each subsequent performance. The blender (or conductor) has similar challenges in the form of differences between casks and the longer-term evolution of a distillery's character.

One way of getting around this is by diversifying the blend. A blend doesn't need to contain more than two whiskies. However, if one member of a two-man band drops dead, the music will not sound the same. But one fewer violinist in a symphony orchestra is more difficult to detect. The art of blending is about fine balance, and about ensuring that sufficient stocks are available to produce the same results year-on-year. The raspberry jam nuance that came from a set of Glenfarclas casks last year might herald Glen Elgin the following year. Hedging your bets on many distilleries grants a kind of insurance policy on the longevity of the flavour profile of the blend.

But with a great number of barrels comes a great responsibility. Managing a blending program is one of the most complex tasks in the industry, since the style and quality of future stocks is difficult to guarantee. The formula for any given blend must be constantly adjusted to accommodate a fluctuation in character of the component single malts. It's like continually proposing new questions to an answer that must remain the same. It's the job of the master blender to smooth out any surprises that might come out of the casks of the component malts and to ensure that those malts play nicely together.

Aeneas MacDonald wrote of blending in 1930:

'Whiskies are capricious, sensitive creatures; they are not to be flung at one another like goats. Rather are they to be compared to fillies which are highly likely to land iron heels in the belly of the too-forward stallion. They must grow accustomed to one another and, unless they have been carefully chosen, no amount of time will persuade them to live together in amity.'

The grain-whisky component of a blend typically makes up 20–60% of the liquid. It's this light canvas that acts as a playground for the more boisterous malt whiskies to mingle. All of the big blending houses are owned by large corporations, whose empires may span multiple grain-whisky distilleries – factories, in essence, that pump out the necessary grain whisky to fulfil the blender's need. There's nothing particularly wrong with grain whisky, but hardly any of it finds its way into a bottle, and when it does, it's usually an independent merchant. The same big companies will also have investments in malt whisky distilleries, which also helps to guarantee the longevity of the blend by controlling quality right from the start of the process. It's easy to forget nowadays, with all the romance and intrigue of single malt whisky, that over 90% of the whisky consumed in the world is blended. Indeed, even the most prestigious of distilleries in Scotland will usually make some contribution towards blends that are owned by their parent company. Diageo, for example, at the time of writing owns and operates around 28 malt distilleries in Scotland, and all except one (Oban) contribute whisky to the Diageo blend portfolio. Oban is a very popular whisky in the US and has a relatively small production run, so all stock is bottled as malt whisky. But even some of Diageo's most prestigious malts (Lagavulin, Talisker and Clynelish) will still roll up their sleeves and help tow the blending line. Around one-third of Diageo's malt distilleries don't even have official malt whisky bottlings – almost all of their product is used in the Johnnie Walker, J&B and Bell's blends.

A big part of managing a warehouse of stock is tapping casks for samples and sending them to the lab for testing and tasting. A blender's room is full of such samples, and they act like stethoscopes, probing the lifeblood of each cask and monitoring its progress to perfect maturation. The decisions made in blending rooms are then escalated up to

huge proportions, where tiny quantities of this and that may become many hundreds of thousands of litres/quarts in the large-scale composition of the whisky. This is why it is said that the blender's nose is the most valuable asset Scotch whisky possesses, because it is that one single organ that determines the bottle contents of millions of bottles across the world.

Blending is common practice in Canada, and if you were to go back 20 years, you'd find that almost all of the whisky there was blended. Although they are not awarded a reputation for it, the Canadian blenders are some of the best blenders in the game. I think they deserve this accolade because they blend not just different-aged whiskies, but also different new-make whiskies prior to ageing. This amounts to what I can only describe as blending in 3D, where proportions must be calculated both before and after maturation, forcing the blender to pre-empt flavour characteristics before they come in to existence – like predicting that a group of children will be friends before some of them have even been born.

RIGHT This blended Scotch is a recreation of abandoned cases of whisky shipped to Antarctica in 1907 by the explorer Ernest Shackleton to fortify his 'Nimrod' expedition.

FILTERING, COLOURING AND STRENGTH

FILTERING

All whisky will undergo some kind of filtration before being bottled. It can be as simple as a mechanical filter (steel, cellulose or nylon mesh) to remove small pieces of wood particles that might have detached themselves from the inside of the cask. Other methods of filtration are also sometimes incorporated to do a more rigorous job.

Some whiskies are charcoal-filtered using 'activated' charcoal, which is carbon that has been treated with oxygen. These lightweight black granules are unique and unrivalled in their surface-area-to-mass ratio – a single gram can have a surface area in excess of 500 square meters (5,382 sqaure feet)! The more surface, the better the chance that large impure molecules hold on or 'adsorb' to the mass of the charcoal. This can be a good or bad thing, since charcoal is not great at discriminating between 'bad' and 'good' flavour molecules. Either way, it has been used in spirits' production for over two centuries, and is important for vodka, where flavour-free is often the goal.

Tennessee whiskies are known for their use of the Lincoln County Process, which sees the white-dog whisky filtered through sugar maple charcoal before ageing. The idea here is that the filtering removes impurities present in the distillate but retains the cask flavour, since no aggressive filtering takes place after ageing (the exception to this rule is Jack Daniel's Gentleman Jack, which undergoes filtering both before and after ageing. Incidentally, the Prichard's Distillery in Tennessee does not conform to the Lincoln County Process.

Many whiskies undergo additional filtering to remove impurities that might affect the clarity of the product. A cloudiness or haze can form in bottled whisky if it is subjected to particularly cold storage conditions, or if served over ice or from the freezer. This is caused by big fatty acids and long-chain esters that come out of solution when the liquid becomes too cold – like covert jellyfish emerging from the ether. The same effect can be seen when pastis or absinthe are diluted with water: suddenly the oils that were previously hidden emerge from suspension.

Cloudiness can also be a sign of a potentially dangerous product, but assuming you are assured of the provenance of the bottle, it's absolutely nothing to worry about. Most of the time the haze will disappear when the bottle is transferred to a warm environment, and it doesn't occur at all in spirits above 46% ABV.

Many producers choose to chill-filter their product before bottling to remove haze-causing particles, deemed to be off-putting to consumers. As the name implies, the whisky is chilled down below 0°C/32°F (and sometimes as low as -12°C/10°F) before passing through a mechanical filter, which removes the guilty particles and leaves the whisky perfectly bright and clear.

Not everyone agrees that chill-filtering has a positive impact on quality, however. While it may be a good way of removing haze, many producers label their product as non-chill-filtered, believing that process removes mouthfeel as well as precious flavour-giving components of the whisky. These tend to be single malt whiskies from Scotland and Japan, but there are a few barrel-proof bourbons that forego filtering, too.

96

COLOURING

For most of you, I'm sure the idea of colouring a whisky seems somewhat absurd. Indeed, if you're brave enough to broach the subject of *artificial* (I'll come back to why I've chosen to put the word in italics shortly) colouring with whisky aficionados, your best bet is to scope out the exits. After all, adding colouring to good-quality single malt, expensive blended whisky, or even Irish pot-still whiskey is hardly necessary, right?

Distiller's caramel, or E150a, as it is also known, is used widely to keep the colour of whiskies consistent and to assist with grading colour according to the age statement of different expressions. This may not seem important to all of us, but to a lot of consumers there is still an association between colour, age and quality. It's a difficult association to overcome for the best of us, and I think that many of us, while perhaps not actually deeming it a fault, will find something to talk about when a 30-year-old single malt is paler in colour than a 25-year-old expression. Given the fickle nature of wood, this sort of thing is not only possible, but actually pretty commonplace.

E150a sounds a lot worse than it actually is. By definition, it is caramel colouring obtained through the heating and caramelization of carbohydrates (sugar). So it is, in fact, just caramel. E150a has no sweetness to it, though, since the process is carefully controlled so as to caramelize all of the available sugars, resulting in a very thick black syrup. By itself the flavour is bitter, if anything, and a little goes a very long way here. A pinprick of caramel is enough to muddy a sink-full of water. For those who believe it can be detected on the tongue, I would happily challenge them. There have been a good number of tests conducted in the past where E150a has been added to water, and only in higher concentrations could it be detected – and that's water we're talking about, not whisky.

I am personally not against the use of caramel for the purpose of uniformity. I do believe it should be stipulated on the bottle, however. What does interest me is the effect that darkening a liquid, with no detectable change to its taste, might have on our flavour perception of the whisky. In other words, do darker whiskies taste of darker things through the power of association alone? In the past, some blenders have broken the trust of the magic circle and revealed caramel as the secret to 'bringing together' a blend. Perhaps it's a darker hue that, in part, cements the relationship between some whiskies.

Oh, and by the way, no colouring is permissible in American whiskey.

STRENGTH

One final consideration, and it's an important one, is the strength at which the product is bottled. I always looked upon the strength of a whisky as a gauge of how much enjoyment I was likely to get from the bottle (higher is better by the way), and how distorted my face would become when I sipped it. Stupid as it sounds, both factors are pertinent, if perhaps not for those reasons.

Cask-strength whisky provides a stronger connection to the production process of the whisky by removing additional (unnecessary some would argue) steps. It also allows the end user (you) a greater control over how the whisky is consumed, by giving you the freedom to dilute it as you see fit... or not at all. Some cask-strength single malt whiskies can top 60% ABV, which is half as strong again as a typical bottle of blended whisky; a 50ml/1¾ fl. oz. dram of Glenfarclas 105, for example, would require 25ml/1 fl. oz of water to take the dram down to 40%. Some bourbons are known to top 70% ABV, an achievement only possible through racked warehousing, or through strict humidity control. The sought-after George T. Stagg release from Buffalo Trace Distillery is one of the strongest that I have come across; the 2007 vintage weighed in at 72.4% ABV – you don't want to see the face that I make at that stage.

How and when whisky is diluted prior to bottling is likely to affect the final flavour of the product. Logic tells us that adding a flavourless liquid to a flavoursome liquid would result in a linear curtailing of flavour in the flavoursome liquid. Exothermic reactions take place when water and alcohol are mixed, and it's likely that there are some changes in perception of sugar and esters based on whether the product was diluted before bottling or during bottling.

There is, like it or not, a certain association between strength and quality. This goes back some years, and the cynic in me would argue that as long as there have been distilled spirits, there has been someone lurking in the shadows with a jug of water eager to dilute the quality and line their pocket. I have seen evidence of one Scottish tradition, similar to the famous 'tequila worm' (which is actually neither a worm nor found in tequila) whereby a fledgling distillery would bottle a small snake with their first run of liquor – the idea being that the successful preservation of the reptile gave assurances to would be buyers of the product's fortitude. The practice reminds me of something that W. C. Fields once said: 'Always carry a small flagon of whisky in case of a snakebite... and furthermore always carry a small snake.'

Some will find high-strength whisky enjoyable and others will recoil at the thought of it – the decision is yours. But more than that, the bottling strength of a whisky can have a big impact on the flavour, too. Alcohol does strange things to our sensory equipment, even though it has little flavour itself. An increase of only 1–2% can be the difference between dark/bittersweet chocolate and milk chocolate flavours, or marzipan and bitter almonds. Higher-strength bottlings offer more scope to play around with this kind of thing by exploring a whisky through different degrees of hydration.

The final factor to consider is price. With a high alcohol percentage comes a high price tag, since it costs the producer more to make it and in most countries it is subject to higher rates of tax. It's easy to forget this when looking at the lofty price tags of some whiskies, and if you're the kind of person who cuts your whisky back with a good splash of water, it's sometimes nice to look at that 70cl/24 fl. oz. bottle as 170cl/57 fl. oz. instead – it makes parting with your money that little bit easier!

THE SCIENCE OF WHISKY FLAVOUR

To understand where a whisky's flavour is derived from is an understanding of whisky-making itself. I am quite persistent when it comes to discovering the inner workings of a problem, but I think of it as a wonderful thing that, even given the extraordinary technological advances, we are essentially shooting in the dark when it comes to building a whisky recipe with the aim of a specific result. There are of course stages of production that we can manipulate to affect certain outcomes, and these are covered in the production sections. But the act of truly picking and choosing a highly specific flavour profile of a whisky remains in the hands of whisky blenders – and it's a likely contributor to the success of blended whiskies. Those people in the past who have established a new distillery from scratch have all faced a uniquely daunting prospect – limited control over the final outcome of the product and no guarantee that it will even be to their own tastes. The good news comes in the shape of hindsight. Even though we lack the ability to truly control flavour, we do have the luxury of looking back on it, acknowledging it, and working out where it came from.

SUBJECTIVE FLAVOUR

We are all born with more or less the same sensory apparatus. Women tend to have a slightly better sense of smell than men, and some people have a better or worse sense of taste than others, which can be distinguished by the concentration of papillae on the surface of the tongue. Don't fret just yet if you believe yourself to be near the bottom of the sensory gene pool – a huge chunk of our ability to detect flavour comes from developing a good flavour dictionary. Your flavour dictionary is like a reference manual for everything that you taste and smell, but it also behaves like a thesaurus by matching some flavours with others and building up associations. The flavour dictionary is set in stone; for example, raspberry tastes likes raspberry because it contains naturally occurring esters, aldehydes, sugars and acids that make up the raspberry flavour. The flavour thesaurus, on the other hand, is an ever-evolving entity, edited and rewritten according to the things that we eat and drink together. If you fed me raspberries and mushrooms together every day for a year, it's fair to say that I would establish an association between the two that is unique to me (since it's doubtful anyone else would pair the two). Some of us have bigger dictionaries than others and we all possess a different copy of the thesaurus – remember that.

Having the dictionary alone is great for appreciating flavour, but to share your joy in flavour, you also need the necessary experience to articulate it. Describing flavour to another person can often feel like describing a piece of music. It's hardly surprising, since both music and flavour are, to an extent, subjective to the individual; I would struggle to describe a piece of classical music accurately to an orchestra conductor, since that person possesses a wealth of musical awareness that is absent to me. I simply lack the hard-earned tools to pick it apart and convey my meaning.

You may hear experts sometimes describe aromas with fantastical language that makes no real sense – marshmallow oil, bee farts and rainbow fur randomly spring to mind – but imaginary smells and creative language are some of the most enjoyable things about discovering flavour, and specifically flavour in whisky. Importantly, these seemingly fanciful

1995 山崎蒸溜所
カスクNo.5R70190

ABOVE The flavour of Japanese whisky regularly walks a fine line between powerful distinction and subtle nuance.

else around you. You are unique, and like everyone else in the world, you are furnished with a multitude of flavour-detecting mechanisms that have been tuned to a rare state of perfection.

THE FLAVOUR OF WHISKY

The range of flavours in whisky is broad, and even though this book uses hundreds of different words to describe whisky flavour, the category itself is for the most part confined to a few key flavour groups. An example of this would be the aroma of smoke, which is prevalent in some single malt whiskies. Anyone who has ever smelled smoke, be it on a barbecue, bonfire, or even a burning building, should be able to detect the aroma of smoke in a whisky from the Laphroaig Distillery on Islay. An example of a less-common aroma would be vegetal, which could possibly feature in a particularly sulphurous whisky, but is less likely to feature in the vocabulary of this book.

Broadly speaking, we can separate whisky flavour into ten groups: fruity, floral, cereal, sulphury, nutty, musty, woody, spicy and smoky. Later, we will tackle the subject of which stage in the whisky-making process these different families of flavours are derived from. First, let us discuss how these families interact with each other to create a flavour image.

In some whiskies you may find a distinct representation of one these ten flavour camps: a strong generic fruity smell, for example. It could be that the fruitiness is more specific, like apples or pears. It even be that you can distinguish the type of apple, or its condition, be it freshly cut and green, or baked and red. In others, there may be a broader representation of five or more flavour camps and it's here that it often becomes tricky to differentiate between flavours.

I like to think of distinguishing flavour like having multiple stories read to you at the same time. If you only have one story to follow it is easy to focus on the plot and to understand it. But if you have three, or five or ten books being read to you simultaneously, perhaps different

descriptions say something about the emotional and spiritual impact of the spirit, alongside that of flavour. Communicating it is a big part of it. Practice is the key to nailing your own communication – not such a bad thing when it comes to delicious whisky! It's through practice and continuous referral to our ever-growing flavour dictionary that we can begin to communicate our findings about individual liquids.

Given the breadth of flavours out there and the infinitely complex associations that are strung together in our minds, it should come as no surprise when I tell you that people, even experts, often disagree on flavour. It's not down to stubbornness or arrogance that this happens (generally), but rather an inconsistency between our flavour thesauruses and the vocabulary we use to express them.

The point is: don't worry if you find it difficult to express your opinion on a whisky, and don't worry if your experience is different to that of someone

HOW WHISKY IS MADE

volumes, it is impossible to keep track of all of them at once. This is often the case with a complex whisky. You can recognize that there are multiple interweaving stories that are being told in the glass and the overall perception is that of rich and varied information, but only when you focus on one flavour plot at a time can you begin to distinguish the subtleties of the tale. The situation can become even more complex when you realize that some characters can appear in multiple stories. In flavour terms, this means that many aromatic molecules crop up in multiple flavour camps. An example would be benzaldehyde, which is most strongly represented by the aroma of almonds, but is also present in apples, apricots and cherries.

Whatever form the aromas take, it comes down to your own personal preference as to whether the positive characteristics combine to significantly outweigh the negative (if any). Many books and magazines put a great emphasis on the grading of whisky through quantitative tastings. While I don't agree with these practices, it's fine to do that if the end goal is a long list of numbers. For me, my assessment of a whisky is done on a drink-by-drink basis and relies on my enjoyment of the liquid at that time, for whatever reason I deem fit.

WHERE THE FLAVOUR COMES FROM

Here is yet another subject that is open to debate – where exactly does the flavour of whisky come from? On the face of it, the answer is simple, as it comes from the three ingredients used to make it: grain, water and wood. Some people may also wish to include yeast as one of whisky's ingredients, especially given all the flavourful compounds that we associate with fermentation. But yeast imparts no direct flavour into whisky; it merely works with the sugars, salts and acids already present in the wort to create new weird and wonderful molecules. In a sense, yeast is no more an ingredient than a mash tun is.

The distillation process further develops these flavours and then goes on to select them through the type of still used and the way that it is managed. Finally the barrel mellows and flavours the liquid through oxidation, through the extraction of harsher flavours and through the infusion of its own. Below I have listed the ingredients and equipment used to make whisky, and how much I believe they contribute towards flavour.

WATER
No effect on whisky flavour other than in the quality used to cut the spirit to bottling strength.

VARIETY OF BARLEY
Negligible effect on flavour.

STEEPING, MALTING AND KILNING
The exact timing and subsequent kilning after germination can affect the build-up of enzymes and carbonyls that can hang around and affect flavour later down the line.

PEAT
Peat is potentially a big portion of flavour contribution, depending on the level to which the barley is peated. Smokiness from peat-drying can be transmitted in various ways into the final product, from phenolic iodine, almost medicinal smoke, through to sweet BBQ, roasted meat, sooty chimney and grilled fish.

RIGHT The rigorous recording of every production stage is the best way to understand where flavour in the final product is likely to have come from.

MASHING

More likely to affect flavour based on how the barley is agitated during mashing and how the wort is filtered out afterwards. Traces of insoluble organic compounds can go on to affect fermentation and distillation character.

YEAST AND FERMENTATION

Critical in the formation of higher alcohols, fatty acids, aldehydes and esters, which all play a critical role in the character of the new-make spirit and beyond. The yeast strain, temperature and pH of the wash will affect the outcome.

SHAPE OF THE STILL, THE CONDENSER AND THE METHOD OF FIRING

Direct-firing affects density of the resulting new make and the potential formation of other flavours during distillation through caramelization and Maillard reactions. The use of a worm tub over a shell-and-tube condenser will make for a more sulphurous and meaty spirit. The shape of the still and the degree of reflux will determine how much of copper's catalyzing affects are leveraged into the new make. Greater levels of reflux are the catalyst for further breakdown of heavier compounds.

HOW THE STILL IS RUN AND THE SPIRIT CUT

How rapidly or gently the still is run can affect the heaviness of the spirit, again in relation to reflux. The cut will determine exactly which flavour components that have been generated thus far make it on the next stage.

BARREL AGEING AND FINISHING

Naturally, ageing has a far greater effect the longer the spirit spends in cask. The type of wood, condition of wood, size of cask, charring or toasting level, temperature of storage and many other factors will play a part, however. Oxidative effects converts alcohols into aldehydes, which in turn convert to fruit esters. Extractive effects cause reactions between hemicellulose in the wood and fatty acids in the spirit, softening and integrating the product. Infusion adds vanillin, tannin, spice and nutty flavours (from lignin) in various degrees to barrel-aged spirits.

CATEGORIZING
WHISKIES

AMERICAN

On the face of it, the classification of American whiskey seems like a simple affair, but delve a little deeper, and you'll find that it's not the case. Each category has its own subtle differences and it's only once you start to list them all down (American, Straight, Bourbon, Straight Bourbon, Kentucky Straight Bourbon… the list goes on), that you begin to realize how complex it really is. The problem is compounded by slightly different laws on labelling between the USA and Europe. For the sake of simplicity, and my own sanity, I have chosen the American take on things in the following sections.

The trick to understanding the American whiskey categories is to understand the hierarchy of terms, and to remember that as the category is further refined, it continues to incorporate the requirements of its parent. For example, *Kentucky Straight Bourbon* needs to meet certain requirements, as well as the requirements of *Straight Bourbon*, *Bourbon* and *Whiskey* itself.

To be sold as *Whiskey* in the USA, the spirit must be made from grain and must be distilled to no more than 95% ABV. It must also have been aged in oak containers, but there is no minimum time restriction for this, or guidance on barrel size and charring or toasting. You could simply give the spirit a swirl in an oak egg cup and call it Bourbon Whiskey.

No additives, including caramel colouring, may be added to whiskey made in America, with Blended American Whiskey being the exception to the rule.

The label must list the state in which the product was made.

BOURBON WHISKEY

Bourbon can be made anywhere in the USA, but most common is Kentucky Bourbon (typically *Straight*). Bourbon has no minimum ageing requirements, but it must be aged in charred new American oak containers with the spirit entering the cask at no more than 62.5% ABV.

All Bourbon whiskey must be made from a minimum of 51% corn in its mash bill and distilled to no higher than 160 proof (80% ABV). Many feature mash bills of up to 80% corn, however, with the remainder of the space being inhabited by rye and/or wheat and malted barley. Bourbon is not permitted to be distilled above 80% ABV: a measure put in place to retain the character of the cereals.

Bourbon aged for under three years may not be called Bourbon whiskey in the EU, but can be called simply 'Whiskey'.

RYE, WHEAT & MALT

Rye follows exactly the same rules as Bourbon except that it must be derived from a mash bill comprising a minimum of 51% rye cereal. There are currently six Straight Rye distilleries, including Anchor,

RIGHT Jim Beam White Label is a Kentucky Straight Bourbon Whiskey, which means it meets the minimum requirements of a whiskey, as well as those of the sub-categories, 'straight', 'Bourbon' and 'Kentucky'.

LEFT George Dickel choose to spell whisky with no 'e', which, interestingly, is the chosen spelling as set out in the US FDA whisky regulations. Whisky and Whiskey are both permitted, however.

BELOW Note that this White Dog from Buffalo Trace Distillery does use the word 'whiskey' in the small print, which means it must have been matured, if only for a brief moment, in an oak container.

LEFT The term 'sour mash', as made famous by the Jack Daniel's brand, is neither a legally recognised term nor a process unique to the Jack Daniel's brand.

BELOW Beam's Eight Star looks similar to Four Roses at first glance, but closer inspection tells us that Beam's is in fact a blend of only 20–50% straight whiskies, and neutral grain spirit.

which uses 100% malted rye. Wheat whiskey follows exactly the same rules as rye, in that the product must be made from a minimum of 51% wheat. Rather interestingly, malt whiskey (like rye and wheat) needs only to be made from 51% malted barley, or more.

CORN

Corn whiskey must be made from a minimum of 80% corn and distilled to no more than 160 proof (80% ABV). No ageing is required, but if the product is aged, it must be in either uncharred casks or, as is more common, refill casks. This prevents the product from sitting in both the *Bourbon* and *Corn* categories at the same time.

STRAIGHT

Whiskey labelled as 'Straight' must be aged for a minimum of two years in oak barrels. The 'Straight' designation is usually, but not exclusively, coupled with a parent category, i.e. *Kentucky Straight Bourbon*, or *Straight Rye*.

Where *Straight* is applied, and the whiskey is aged for under four years, it must display its age on the bottle; if it's aged above four years, it is optional. It's a good incentive for producers to hit the four-year mark. There is one exception to the Straight classification – when applied to corn whiskey, uncharred casks can be used for the usual minimum ageing time of two years.

KENTUCKY WHISKEY

Obviously this stuff needs to be produced in Kentucky, but other than that, it needs only to adhere to the requirements of an American whiskey. Almost all whiskies produced in Kentucky are Straight Bourbons, however, and even the ones that aren't, usually adhere to the Bourbon rules, if not the Straight.

TENNESSEE WHISKEY

Tennessee is essentially a Straight Bourbon, but two things make it distinct. Firstly, the fact that it is made in Tennessee (which in itself does not prohibit it from being a Bourbon), and secondly, that it is filtered through 3 metres/10 feet of maple sugar charcoal before ageing, also known as the Lincoln County Process. It's this process that makes it a Tennessee Whiskey and prevents it from being either Straight, or Bourbon. The exception to this rule is Prichard's Tennessee Whiskey, which does not conduct the Lincoln County Process after being granted a legal exemption.

BOTTLED IN BOND

Bottled in Bond is a term that crops up from time to time in American whiskey. It's a little like the single malt of the whiskey world.

Federal regulations state that a Bottled-in-Bond Whiskey must be the product of one distillation season in one distillery. It also must be aged for a minimum of four years and bottled at a minimum of 50% ABV. Otherwise, Bottled-in-Bond Whiskey follows the same barrel and distillate strength regulations as Straight Whiskey.

AMERICAN BLENDED

Whisky designated as *blended* in the US must contain a minimum of 20% *Straight Whiskey* (blended or otherwise). Other than that, you can add neutral spirits or younger whiskies to the mix. If the product has Bourbon, Rye, Wheat or Malt in its name, it must then contain a minimum of 51% of that particular designation of whiskey. This does not mean the cumulative mash bill is made up of 51% rye – in a *Blended Rye*, for example, it could be as low as 26%.

SCOTCH

The term *Scotch Whisky* by itself is a bit useless, since any given product must reside in one of the sub-categories listed

below. But broadly speaking, Scotch whisky must abide by the following rules (according to the Scotch Whisky Regulations 2009): it must be made in Scotland from water, cereal and yeast only, whereby sugars are obtained through malt enzymes (diastase). Mashing, fermentation and distillation must take place in the distillery and it must be distilled to less than 94.8% ABV. It must then be aged in oak casks no bigger than 700 litres/739 quarts, for a minimum of three years. Before the three years are up, it is known simply as 'British New-Make Spirit'. Plain caramel colouring may be added.

SCOTCH SINGLE MALT WHISKY

Single Malt Whisky must be made from 100% malted barley, but the barley can be grown and malted anywhere in the world. It must be distilled a minimum of two times in a copper pot still; you can distill three times (like Auchentoshan), or even more, but it's not all that common. As with all Scotch Whisky, the maximum permitted distillate strength is 94.8% ABV, but most Single Malt Whiskies run off at 65–75% ABV.

Ageing must take place in Scotland, but not necessarily on the site of the distillery. Obviously most bottlings are much older than the required three years, but it is possible to get young whiskies that exhibit a lot more distillery character than the 12-year+ drams most of us are familiar with. During the period in which the whisky is kept in barrels, it's stored in a government-bonded warehouse.

As with all types of Scotch, the age statement on the bottle must refer to the youngest whisky in the bottle. Vintage Single Malt Whisky poses another challenge, as it can be a little confusing when deciphering its age. These whiskies are permitted to list only one year on the label, and it can be either the 'distilled on', or 'bottled on' date, accompanied by an age statement. As of 2009, all Single Malt Whisky must be bottled in Scotland.

SCOTCH BLENDED MALT WHISKY

As the name eloquently suggests, this type of whisky is a blend of two or more single Malt Whiskies. In the past, Blended Malt has gone by the title 'Vatted Malt' and 'Pure Malt', but 2009 legislation put a stop to that. It is usually big, bold and not all that often seen, since most people would rather drink a Blended Scotch or a Single Malt rather than something in-between. As is the norm, the age statement on a Blended Malt refers to the youngest whisky. Johnnie Walker Green Label is a great example of a smoky Blended Malt (partly down to the inclusion of both Talisker and Caol Isla in the blend), and I also love Compass Box's Spice Tree, which spent a brief spell out of production over a dispute with the Scotch Whisky Association.

SINGLE GRAIN SCOTCH WHISKY

Like Single Malt, Single Grain must be the product of one single distillery, but it can be made from any combination of malted barley and other un-malted cereals (but not other malted cereals). It is typically produced in a column still, which produces a much lighter spirit than a pot still. Single Grain Whisky is seldom bottled for consumption on its own, and almost all of the Single Grain Whisky in Scotland is used in blends.

If you are in the market for a bottle, check out Cameron Brig, which makes up the backbone of many famous blends.

BLENDED SCOTCH WHISKY

Despite the growing demand for Single Malt in the past 20 years, blended Scotch makes up over 90% of the global Scotch Whisky sales today. It must be made from at least one Single Malt and one Single Grain Whisky. As far as I am aware, there are no blends that contain more than one Single Grain Whisky, but many contain over 30 Single Malts.

ABOVE AND RIGHT Age statements aren't essential for Scotch whisky, but without one the consumer can only be assured that the whisky is at least 3 years old.

LEFT AND BELOW Johnnie Walker 'Pure Malt', also known as 'Green Label' is a rarity now; unlike the ubiquitous Black Label, it was a blend of malt whiskies only.

IRISH

The rules that govern Irish Whiskey are much broader than those of Scotch or American. The Irish Whiskey Act of 1980 set out three basic requirements for Irish Whiskey: firstly, Irish Whiskey can be made from any combination of cereal so long as it is 'saccharified by the diastase of malt' (i.e. there must be some malt used); secondly, it must be distilled to an alcoholic strength of less than 94.8% ABV; and thirdly, it must be aged for a minimum of three years in wooden casks.

The broad scope of this law means that any additional information on the label, such as 'Pot Still', 'Single Malt', or 'Single Grain', is in fact meaningless, since their definition is covered by the act. These terms are, of course, familiar in the world of Scotch Whisky, and one can only trust that they refer to similar quality standards when used on Irish labels.

LEFT AND BELOW The loose and liberal Irish whiskey rules are set to change in the near future, while Canadian whisky regulations still permit the use of flavourings, even though most new distilleries take no advantage of it.

CANADIAN

There is a common perception harboured by aficionados that Canadian whisky is largely unregulated and that the kids are essentially left to run amok. On the face of it, Canadian whisky follows similar rules to that of Scotch Grain Whisky, besides the obvious fact that it must be made in Canada, that is. According to the Canadian Whisky (Food and Drugs Act 1985), Canadian Whisky must be made from the diastase (enzymes) of malt. It cannot be distilled above 94% ABV; colouring is permitted; and it must be aged in 'small wood' containers (maximum of 700 litres/740 quarts) for no fewer than three years. Where Canadian Whisky differs from other styles is in the sanction of up to 9.09% 'flavouring' that may be added to it, which can be in the form of Sherry, Port, wine, or even other spirits. The exacting figure of 9.09% is equal to one part out of 11, or one part flavouring for every 10 parts whisky.

It would be frowned upon, however, if you slopped a load of melted chocolate

into the vat. Regardless of flavouring, the product must 'possess the aroma, taste and character generally attributed to Canadian Whisky'.

RYE

Whiskies labelled as 'Rye' in Canada contain a proportion of rye in their mash bill, but typically only 5–15%. If they are to be exported to the USA, the 'rye' must be removed from the label, unless the product meets the minimum (51%) rye requirements required by US law.

PART THREE
BLENDS & COCKTAILS

How to Enjoy Whisky

Now listen: I enjoy a dram or a shot as much as the next person. The fact that I have spent so many pages exploring the history, science, production and nuances of whisky is testament to this fact. During the making of this book I sampled over 1,000 whiskies, and some of them benefitted greatly from a splash of water to awaken the serpent and reveal the more elusive elements of the spirit. For many people, water or ice are the only modifiers to be granted an audience with a glass of whisky; anything else is considered devil worship. For the real purists among us, the mere suggestion of water can be too much to stomach, confirming the old adage that there are only two things that a Highlander likes naked, and one of them is his whisky.

I have witnessed first hand the mood of a Scottish bar turning sour at the suggestion of mixing a malt whisky, but the Irish don't seem to care how you consume their whiskey, as long as you consume it. Lots of it. The Japanese take a more zen-like approach to things – for them, it's not what you mix whisky with, but rather how you mix it. In the US, rules about bourbon consumption are scarce, but it tends to fall into one of two categories: mixed and sweet, or straight from the bottle.

The truth is that the best way to enjoy whisky is the way that you most prefer it.

Ignore the rule book and don't listen to the purists. Enjoyment cannot be learned or acquired; it's entirely subjective, so do it your own way – or don't do it at all.

Indeed, even the people who make the stuff cannot agree on the best way to analyse whisky, or to enjoy it. I have taken part in tastings with whisky distillers and blenders at which all samples were diluted by 50%, and others at which samples were served strictly at bottle or cask strength only, and covered for a minimum of 30 minutes before nosing commences.

My one and only tip for assessing whisky is to ensure that plenty of air flows through your mouth and out of your nose while tasting. This has the effect of carrying a good concentration of the volatile aromatic molecules over your smelling apparatus. It probably won't involve the wine-tasters 'slurp', but might mean a bit of 'swishing' and a lot of creepy heavy-breathing.

In the following section I've included a selection of mixed drinks and preparations that do a good job of celebrating the unique character of whiskies from all over the world. Some are for classic cocktails, and also include a little history and commentary. Others are original recipes or my own take on classic recipes. It's a pretty eclectic selection, but there should be something for everyone.

My Blends

The blending of whisky is something quite close to my own heart – after all, I've made a career out of combining things in an effort to create something greater than the sum of its parts. Blending your own whisky can be a very rewarding experience, but it can also be a waste of good booze if you get it wrong. One of the biggest traps I fall into when blending is knowing where to draw the line and admit that the mixture in front of you is doomed to fail, that no amount of sprucing up with other whiskies can save it. When that happens, remember you can always use a failed blend in cocktails or highballs – a good way of covering up a blending blunder!

Over the next few pages I have included five tried-and-tested blend formulas you can rely on. The proportions I've used give a good indication of the balance between grain and malt whisky in a typical blend, and also highlight some of the malts that add key aromatic and taste parameters to my own formulas. You can use them as they are, or take them as inspiration for your own creations. Most commercially sold blends are made up of anything from 20–60% grain whisky; my blends are at the lower end of this scale, which gives the malts an opportunity to sing a little bit louder.

You might also notice that most of my blends contain only five or six whiskies, as opposed to the 20-plus that sometimes make up popular blends. As with cocktails, I generally prefer to keep things simple, for several reasons. Firstly, it's unlikely that anyone will be rushing out to buy 20 different bottles of whisky just because I say they combine nicely. Secondly, the likes of you and me don't need to hedge our bets with a wide range of blended whiskies in the hope that one or two will become popular, like the commercial distilleries do. And thirdly, I honestly don't think that good blends need countless whiskies to taste good. Most malt whisky tastes great as it is, so why bother condemning a good dram to obscurity by spreading it too thin?

All the blends except Grand Old Lustre contain some grain whisky, which forms the backbone of the liquid. Grain whisky is becoming more readily available, but it is not something you're likely to find on a supermarket shelf. Cameron Brig is a grain whisky product that shouldn't prove too hard to track down, but if you are really struggling you can try using an Irish whiskey such as Bushmills Original (which contains a large proportion of grain spirit) as your grain base.

The first blend, Highland, is a typical balanced blend of whiskies that aims to highlight all that is great about Scotch whisky. The other four blends are more specific and explore specific families of flavour; they are unnatural and blatant abuses of the blender's art in an attempt to make something really special. These blends make interesting cocktail ingredients, too, since they provide a highly focused flavour to the drink, allowing for fine tuning by balancing the other ingredients.

HIGHLAND BLEND

250 ML/8¾ FL. OZ. CAMERON BRIG

100 ML/3½ FL. OZ. MORTLACH 18-YEAR-OLD
Meatiness, Fruit, Sherry

100 ML/3½ FL. OZ. MACDUFF 16-YEAR-OLD
Green, Mossy

100 ML/3½ FL. OZ. ARDMORE TRADITIONAL
Smoked Fruit

200 ML/7 FL. OZ. TEANINICH 10-YEAR-OLD
Herbal, Grassy

200 ML/7 FL. OZ. LONGMORN 16-YEAR-OLD
Nettle, Oats, Honey

150 ML/5¼ FL. OZ. OBAN 14-YEAR-OLD
Earth, Smoke, Rope

This Highland Blend is what I consider to be a day-to-day drinking blend. It really captures the essence of the whisky-making tradition, and in some ways emulates the classic blends of old. All the whiskies in this blend are from the Scottish Highlands; some are fruity, some are nutty and a couple of them are slightly smoky.

When drinking this blend I am transported to a misty Scottish morning. The air is settled, but moisture fills it and the heather is wet with dew. There's a faint smell of peat bog and the warm fragrance of rotting vegetation underfoot. The effort of walking causes a rush of heat through the bloodstream, which is tempered by the gurgling sound of clear cold water twisting through the glen. From my pocket I produce a hip flask, and this is what's in it.

English Country Garden

300 ML/10½ FL. OZ. CAMERON BRIG

100 ML/3½ FL. OZ. LOCH LOMOND
Esters, Juniper

100 ML/3½ FL. OZ. CLYNELISH 16-YEAR-OLD
Honey, Wood

150 ML/5¼ FL. OZ. CARDHU
Grass, Apple, Pear

150 ML/5¼ FL. OZ. OLD PULTENEY NAVIGATOR
Blackberry, Honey, Rose, Salt

100 ML/3½ FL. OZ. HIGH WEST RENDEZVOUS
Rose, Lychee

50 ML/2 FL. OZ. GLENFARCLAS 30-YEAR-OLD
Allspice, Patchouli, Wood

50 ML/2 FL. OZ. ARDBEG
Smoke, Citrus

Floral, grassy and herbal characteristics are normally best when balanced out by solid wood notes and vanillin. This blend aims to do the complete opposite, however. I wanted the aroma and taste to be as fragrant, sweet and inviting as possible, even if it meant losing balance in the process. This whisky is nothing short of a garden perfume made from ingredients foraged by a six-year-old girl: flowers, grass, herbs, moss, a touch of fruit and busy bees.

This is a wonderful blend to drink with soda, since the bubbles lift some of the floral notes and the dilution serves to heighten the fragrant qualities of the whisky, knocking back any heaviness that manages to slip through.

Scotch Blend III

Fruit & Nut

300 ML/10¹/₂ FL. OZ. CAMERON BRIG

200 ML/7 FL. OZ. LONGMORN 16-Year-Old
Porridge, Apple, Honey

200 ML/7 FL. OZ. DAILUAINE 16-Year-Old
Esters, Fruit cake

100 ML/3¹/₂ FL. OZ. JURA 16-Year-Old
Granola, Hazelnut

100 ML/3¹/₂ FL. OZ. ABERFELDY 21-Year-Old
Fig, Lemon, Wood

100 ML/3¹/₂ FL. OZ. BALBLAIR 1997
Lemon, Mango, Apricot

This was a fun and relatively simple blend to come up with; after all, fruit bowls are fairly consistent from household to household, and the concept is less subjective than others. Imagine a fruit bowl furnished with a selection of your favourite fresh and dried fruit, then select the whiskies that best embody those fruits. The trick is not to get carried away with too many, which can result in a muddy, fruit-salad effect that tastes fruity, but not of any one fruit in particular.

The most common fruits to crop up in malt whisky are plum, apricot, fig, raspberry and apple, but they can take many shapes and forms. Plums, for example, can be fresh, stewed, preserved, folded between pastry, or dried into prunes. In this blend I aimed for a mixture of fresh and dried fruit.

Scotch Blend IV

Sweetshop

500 ML/17½ FL. OZ. GIRVAN NO. 4 APPS GRAIN SPIRIT
Pink prawns/shrimp, Banana candy

50 ML/2 FL. OZ. AULTMORE 15-YEAR-OLD (MASTER OF MALT BOTTLING)
Juicy fruit gum, Banana bread, Krispy Kreme doughnut

200 ML/7 FL. OZ. DEANSTON 19-YEAR-OLD (MASTER OF MALT BOTTLING)
Dr. Pepper, Cinnamon, Buttercream frosting

100 ML/3½ FL. OZ. HIGHLAND PARK 10-YEAR-OLD
Sponge cake, Cherry gum, Menthol

50 ML/2 FL. OZ. GLENCADAM 21-YEAR-OLD
Orange soda, Wood

50 ML/2 FL. OZ. SPRINGBANK CV
Sugared pastry

100 ML/3½ FL. OZ. MACDUFF 15-YEAR-OLD
Cream soda, Lime oil, Moss

One of the most exciting things about whisky is its ability to conjure up childhood memories, especially that of the sweet shop/candy store. There's a whole ton of aromatics in malt whisky that are actually used to flavour candy, such as esters like isoamyl acetate (banana, pear drops) and isobutyl formate (raspberry sherbet), and other compounds like ethyl maltol (candy floss/cotton candy) and benzaldehyde (marzipan). The idea of this blend is to create a whisky that tastes like an all-out sweet shop assault, with that blast of warm candy aroma that hits you when you walk in, accompanied by the almost tangible feeling of sugar in the air and on your skin. All of the whiskies I have used are floral, fruity or sweet, and combined they have a long, syrupy linger.

GRAND OLD LUSTRE

500 ML/17½ FL. OZ. CLYNELISH 16-YEAR-OLD
Wax, Honey, Glue, Wood

100 ML/3½ FL. OZ. TALISKER 18-YEAR-OLD
Mahogany, Tobacco, Chocolate

150 ML/5¼ FL. OZ. ABERFELDY 12-YEAR-OLD
Saddle leather, Honey

250 ML/8¾ FL. OZ. GLENCADAM 21-YEAR-OLD
Caramel, Varnish, Orange

50 ML/2 FL. OZ. GLENFARCLAS 21-YEAR-OLD
Polish, Nectarine, Wood

50 ML/2 FL. OZ. HIGHLAND PARK 40-YEAR-OLD
Oak toast, Tea, Spice

The fifth and final blend is aptly named Grand Old Lustre. It is a combination of whiskies displaying plenty of polished wood, glue and gloss, finesse and age. My good friend Craig Harper describes this kind of whisky as 'like licking a sideboard'. I find this sort of thing delicious: various varieties of wood, from cedar to maple, walnut and, of course, oak, meld together to give a sense of wealth and grandness. Additionally, sweetness and tannin interplay with ethyl acetate, wood spice, nutty Sherry notes, leather and fruit esters to reinforce the notion of a richly furnished stately home.

This is a whisky to be savoured on its own, not because it contains expensive malts (which it does), but because the delicate aromatics that it holds are as fragile as the old furniture it aims to mirror. You'll also notice that there is no grain whisky in this blend; it's a blended malt.

This would be an expensive whisky if it was on sale commercially – the inclusion of Talisker, Highland Park and Glenfarclas make sure of that. Interestingly, though, it would legally only be able to label itself as a 12-year-old, because that is the age of Aberfeldy, the youngest malt in the bottle. But for me it's not the same without the creamy youthfulness that the Aberfeldy bestows, and it goes to show that age statements should never be a mark of quality.

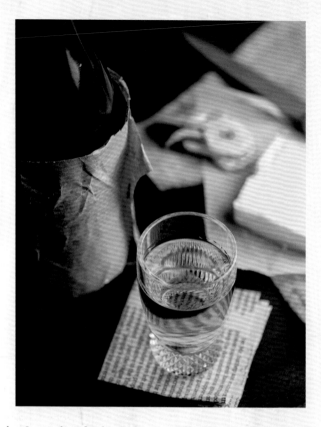

Back when I opened my first bar, Purl, we were lucky enough to ride the crest of an unprecedented creative wave. Ideas for new drinks concepts came to us thick and fast, and while some of them were madcap, hair-brained designs, others had legs and became awesome cocktails that made it onto the list.

One such drink was inspired, in part, by the Boilermaker (see page 124). The concept was based around the ritual (perhaps a loose sense of the word) of American street drinking: that is, the stereotypical bum, clutching a bottle of hooch in a brown paper bag. 'Brown-bagging' is a loophole in the law governing open alcohol containers in public spaces in the US. We thought it would be fun to serve a drink in a bottle wrapped in brown paper, so that the guests would feel as if they were partaking in a barely legal activity while enjoying the drink. If we could have given them a park bench, we would have. The drink itself contained bourbon, apple juice, cardamom and apricot brandy. The bottle was beer-bottle sized and it combined the two parts of the traditional Boilermaker into one not-so-neat package. We sprayed beer onto the brown paper for aromatic effect and served the drink at the table on a square of newspaper in place of a regular napkin.

Around a year later, we were ready for

Beer & Bump

35 ML/1¼ FL. OZ. JACK DANIEL'S OLD NO. 7

200 ML/7 FL. OZ. BUTTER BEER (SEE BELOW)

•

For the Butter Beer:

50 G/3 TABLESPOONS BUTTER

10 G/SCANT 1 TABLESPOON SUGAR

5 G/1 TABLESPOON DRIED BANANA CHIPS

2 G/½ TEASPOON SALT

2 WHOLE CLOVES

1 CARDAMOM POD

2 SAGE LEAVES

500 ML/17 FL. OZ. DARK BELGIAN ALE (LEFFE BRUNE IS GOOD)

•

First, we need to flavour the butter. Melt it in a pan and add all the dry ingredients. Heat gently for 5 minutes, being careful not to burn the butter. Leave to stand for a few minutes, then pour off the clarified part of the butter into a separate bowl, leaving behind the milk solids and all the spices.

Add the clarified butter to the beer and give it a vigorous stir. Seal it in a wide-necked vessel and put it in the fridge for 12 hours. The butter should solidify, allowing you to scoop it off the top. Pass the beer through a fine sieve to remove any extra lumps of butter, then keep in the fridge for up to a week.

Glass: Shot glass and bottle wrapped in brown paper
Garnish: Beer aroma and newspaper square

the second incarnation of the drink, and it was renamed Beer & Bump. This time the drink came in two parts: a shot of Jack Daniel's and a beer-flavoured drink in a bottle. We wanted to serve a 'beer' that was flavoured with ingredients complementary to the Jack. Looking at the flavour profile, we picked out characteristics such as banana, maple, oak and spice. Now the challenge was on to

flavour a suitable beer, one that would complement Jack Daniel's from the get-go, and present the two alongside each other. Here is my updated recipe for Beer & Bump, which I think works a treat. The flavours infused in the beer do a wonderful job of softening the alcohol in the Jack Daniel's, so that the two drinks bounce off one another and beg you to keep on sipping!

BOILERMAKER

1 BOTTLE MILLER LIGHT

25 ML/1 FL. OZ. JIM BEAM WHITE LABEL

•

Serve the beer ice-cold from the fridge, and the bourbon in a short, thick shot glass.
Consume both liquids as you see fit. Make another.

Glass: Shot glass

Many of my American friends would surely argue that the Boilermaker is not a cocktail. And given that the drink normally comprises a shot of bourbon and a bottle of beer, they might be right. However, often the most simple drinking rituals resonate more powerfully through bar culture than complex cocktails.

Popular wisdom tells us that a true Boilermaker should be a shot of bourbon dropped into a glass of beer. The drinker is then required to down the mixture in one. I personally prefer either shooting the bourbon and then sipping the beer, or sipping alternately between the two glasses. The night tends to last a little longer that way, too!

If you're still doubtful as to the cocktail credentials of this fantastic beverage, know this: the drink featured in the 1932 book *The Art of Mixing* by James Wiley and Helene Griffith, albeit under the name Block and Fall (walk a block, fall, walk a block, fall, and so on).

According to the *Oxford English Dictionary*, the term 'boilermaker' was first defined as a steam locomotive engineer almost 100 years previously, in 1834. It seems to make sense that a 'why have one drink when you can have two?' beverage

such as the Boilermaker shares its name with a sweat-stained, coal-smeared grease monkey. There is one tall tale that suggests the name Boilermaker (Beer & Bump) predates the Boilermaker (Gear & Sump). It's a story I'm inclined to disbelieve, since it originates in my home county in the UK and people in those parts are often guilty of a little romanticization.

It's Christmas Eve, 1801, and we're in Camborne, Cornwall. The town's blacksmith, Richard Trivithick, has just finished engineering an early steam engine and plans to test it by driving it up Camborne Hill. The engine, known as the Puffing Devil, comes to a halt outside the local pub, and much celebration ensues, right on through until morning, the choice tipple for the evening being beer and whisky chasers with roast goose. Sadly, the story ends in disaster: the engine was parked up and the boiler allowed to burn dry, resulting in fire and the total destruction of the engine. A powerful reminder of the pitfalls of drinking one too many Boilermakers! Regardless, the story became one of Cornwall's best-loved drinking songs, 'Camborne Hill'.

BLOOD & SAND

35 ML/1¼ FL. OZ. DEWAR'S WHITE LABEL

35 ML/1¼ FL. OZ. CHERRY HEERING LIQUEUR

35 ML/1¼ FL. OZ. MARTINI ROSSO VERMOUTH

35 ML/1¼ FL. OZ. FRESH ORANGE JUICE

•

Shake all the ingredients with ice and strain into a chilled martini glass.

Glass: Martini   **Garnish:** Cherry

This drink was on the menu at the first cocktail bar I worked at. It was my least favourite of all the cocktails we served and I distinctly remember it reminding me of vomit. I came to love it later, however, and more than most I think this drink is a great reflection of its name. Now that I've sold it to you so well, let's discuss its origins and ingredients!

The drink was named after the 1922 Rudolph Valentino film of the same name. It's a silent movie about a bullfighter, which explains the blood and sand connection. Exactly who invented the drink is not known, but the first time the recipe was published, like so many other drinks, was in the 1930 *Savoy Cocktail Book*.

The drink calls for equal parts Scotch, cherry brandy, sweet vermouth and orange juice, which might go some way

towards explaining my initial distaste – these are not ingredients you imagine would marry nicely. Indeed, it would seem that the bartender responsible committed the cardinal sin of mixing drinks by colour rather than flavour, since the vermouth and cherry brandy are both red (blood) and the Scotch and orange juice are both orange (sand). Serendipity should never be underestimated, however – after all, Teflon, plastic and even the colour mauve were all invented by accident! The same luck was granted to the inventor of the Blood & Sand. He was only looking for a nice-coloured drink, and what he ended up with was a fortuitous and flavoursome combination of ingredients. Whisky is the backbone of this drink, but expect acidity, sweetness and big competition between all the powerful aromatics.

PICKLEBACK

50 ML/2 FL. OZ. JAMESON IRISH WHISKEY

50 ML/2 FL. OZ. DILL PICKLE JUICE

•

Pour the two liquids into separate shot glasses. Shoot the whiskey, then the pickle juice.
That's about it!

Glass: Shot glass

I was first introduced to the phenomenon of the Pickleback by James 'Jocky' Petrie of The Fat Duck restaurant. He was sitting at the bar in Purl one evening and after a couple of drinks started raving about a mad drink that combined Irish whiskey and pickle brine. It sounding both disgusting and fascinating, so I immediately sent the barman back out to the shop to buy a jar of dill pickles. Jocky instructed us to pour Irish whiskey into one shot glass and the juice from the dill pickle jar into another. You shoot back the whiskey, then chase it with the sweet-and-sour pickle brine. It was amazing.

So how does it work? It would appear that the intense sweet, sour and saltiness of the pickle juice does a very good job of detracting from the alcohol burn of the whiskey. But not only that, it actually couples nicely with the liquor, leaving a kind of sweet, toffee-apple aftertaste that is far from unpleasant. The ritual is not dissimilar from that of the Tequila Slammer and Sangrita, which achieve much the same thing, albeit with very different flavour combinations.

Now I must confess at this stage to being an Irish Pickleback advocate, which is not necessarily true to the historical roots of the drink. It was T. J. Lynch of NYC bar Breslin who, in 2009, made a Pickleback with Jameson whiskey famous, but it would appear that the practice had been going on with bourbon for at least a year or two before that. According to New York bartender Toby Ceccini (famed for his part in the creation of the Cosmopolitan), the drink was first served to him in 2007 with Old Crow Bourbon at the Bushwick Country Club in the Williamsburg neighbourhood of Brooklyn. It seems that the ritual may have been inspired by a culture of chasing liquor with pickle juice adopted by Texan long-haul truck drivers. The salt supposedly helps keep you hydrated, thus preventing a morning-after trucker headache. Since Texas borders Mexico, it seems plausible that the idea originally came from the Sangrita.

Either way, the quality of the pickle juice is far more important than the quality of the whiskey, since the ritual is designed to clear the palate of low-grade liquor, so choose your pickles wisely!

MALT BLANC

20 ML/¾ FL. OZ. BREWED MILK OOLONG TEA

35 ML/1¼ FL. OZ. DALWHINNE 16-YEAR-OLD

120 ML/4¼ FL. OZ. UNSWEETENED SOY MILK

15 G/1 TABLESPOON WILDFLOWER HONEY (ACCORDING TO TASTE)

•

Brew the tea at 90°C/195°F at a ratio of one part tea to 20 parts water and allow to infuse for 5 minutes. Strain the leaves out and leave to cool. Combine all the ingredients in a cocktail shaker and shake with ice. Remove the ice, then 'dry shake' the liquid to introduce plenty of air. Pour the drink into a tall glass and garnish with a cinnamon stick dusted with icing/confectioners' sugar.

Glass: Sundae
Garnish: Cinnamon stick dusted with icing/confectioners' sugar

This is a drink I invented for L'Aubergaude hotel in Morzine, France. The aim was to create a whisky cocktail that was highly approachable, but that also drew influence from the French Alps. The obvious route was to make a white-coloured drink, which typically means milk, cream or yoghurt, but I wanted to avoid the heaviness of those ingredients so instead opted to use soy milk. Soy milk, and rice milk for that matter, do have a certain affinity with malt whisky, a kind of nutty sweetness that tastes very wholesome and 'of the earth'.

That nutty characteristic led me to the next ingredient: tea. Chilled green tea is a very popular whisky mixer in China, where the almost citrus-like grassiness of the tea lengthens the spirit, but remains sympathetic to its character. Green tea didn't deliver quite the flavour I wanted, though, so I turned to oolong, and more specifically, milk oolong. This particular type of is prized for its milky texture; it's

oily, naturally sweet and not at all bitter when prepared correctly.

The drink required some sweetening, which would improve the texture, and also balance out the dryness of the other ingredients and suppress some of the volatile alcohol characteristics. I quickly found that too much alcohol heat in a milky drink was especially unpleasant – milk shouldn't burn; it simply isn't natural. I settled on wildflower honey, which contributed fruitiness along with its delicate sweet flavour, once again making a good partner to malt whisky.

Speaking of the whisky, I chose Dalwhinnie 16-year-old. There were two good reasons for this, the first being Dalwhinnie's dessert-like qualities of caramel, chocolate and silky vanilla custard. The second, less important but very apt, reason is that Dalwhinnie is Scotland's highest distillery – the perfect choice for a drink named after the highest mountain in Western Europe.

PEAT & MELON

30 ML/1¼ FL. OZ. MORTLACH 16-YEAR-OLD

20 ML/¾ FL. OZ. TALISKER 10-YEAR-OLD

20 ML/¾ FL. OZ. MERLET MELON LIQUEUR

A TINY PINCH OF SALT

•

Stir the whiskies together with ice, the melon liqueur and salt for 1 minute. Strain into a chilled glass and garnish with the rocket/arugula leaf and a small blob of olive oil.

Glass: Tulip glass   **Garnish:** Rocket/arugula leaf and peppery olive oil

Although many of my creations have been inspired by food, I'm always quick to stress that the influence the kitchen has on the bar is not as straightforward as you might think. Taking the essence of a dish – the interplay between ingredients, the sweet and sour balance, the correct use of seasoning – is a tricky art to master, but rewarding when done well.

One of my few truly successful attempts at transforming a food concept into a drink is Peat & Melon, which I created in 2010. The food in question is the delicious Parma ham and melon salad I scoff every time I go to Italy. The genius of the salad is the salty, meaty taste of the ham coupled with the intoxicating, sweet and slightly acidic melon. Salt and sweet are under-recognized bedfellows – where would we be without salted caramel? – and cocktail bartenders are missing a trick by under-using salt in their creations.

It only became possible once Merlet melon liqueur was released. Merlet is the only brand I recognize as coming close to the naturally vibrant melon flavour you find in a ripe honeydew melon. Sure, you could muddle or juice a melon, but that's a total hassle and the chances are your drink will end up cloudy or lumpy – not desirable traits. In short, no other melon liqueur will do, especially not the toxic green one that shall remain nameless. With the melon box ticked, it was time to choose a whisky or whiskies that best represent salty cured ham. This was all about keeping the flavour delicate, but decidedly animal-like.

Whiskies with a meatiness about them tend to be formed from sulphurous new-make spirit. This means minimal copper contact and probably a 'worm tub' condenser. When whisky blenders are looking for meaty, there's one distillery they will always turn to: Dufftown's oldest distillery, Mortlach. The brawn of Mortlach is a powerful backbone to many blends and it was the obvious choice for this drink, but I also needed something a little more funky and salty to provide the spice, fruit and smoke that is also present in Parma ham. For this I turned to Talisker. Made on the Isle of Skye, it is a great example of whisky that has taken a good look at its surroundings, then concentrated them into the bottle. It's peppery, fruity, smoky, and most of all, noticeably salty: perfect for my cocktail.

the world that date back hundreds of years. The archive is strictly closed to the public, but I have on occasion been granted access. It's here that the only known document with John Walker's signature exists.

The archives also record the brewing of Walker's ginger beer. An 1825 stock inventory shows that Walker had two casks for the brewing of fermented ginger beer and a number of bottles intended for its packaging. Thirty years later in 1857, the store still held stocks of ground ginger, whole ginger and preserved ginger, presumably either for general sale or for the production of ginger beer.

Pairing whisky with ginger is nothing new, since the two have a strong affinity with one another, and 'Scotch and dry' is one of the most widely consumed whisky drinks in the world. For my version of Walker's Ginger Brew I have brewed a ginger beer in the traditional manner, with the exception of spiking it with some Johnnie Walker Black Label.

When I visited the Cardhu Distillery in Scotland's Speyside region I was also shown around the Johnnie Walker museum. Cardhu is considered the spiritual home of Walker after it was bought by them back in 1893. While I was being shown around the relics, the discussion moved on to other products that the Walker family had made during the 19th century. John Walker himself started out as a tea blender and grocer, and many of these items continued to be sold, even after the whisky business had taken off. One such product was ginger beer, and when I returned from the trip I got in touch with the Johnnie Walker archives to find out more.

Deep in rural Scotland there is a building housing the largest collection of historical alcohol-related documents in

To do this you need to make a 'ginger beer plant' (GBP), which is basically a living culture of yeast and ginger. The living ingredients are used in a similar way to a sourdough starter for baking, comprising a mixture of ground ginger, sugar, yeast and water which, when left to react, encourages acid build-up through the interaction of the ingredients. The good news is that, just like sourdough, you can keep this culture fed and use it over and over again, marvelling as the flavour develops.

WALKER'S GINGER BREW

1.5 LITRES/1½ QUARTS WATER

10 G/⅓ OZ. SLICED MEDIUM-HOT RED CHILLI

20 G/¾ OZ. FINELY GRATED FRESH GINGER

20 G/¾ OZ. GRATED LEMON ZEST

3 G/½ TEASPOON CREAM OF TARTAR

240 G/1¼ CUPS CASTER/SUPERFINE SUGAR

60 G/2¼ OZ. GBP (SEE BELOW)

240 ML/8½ FL. OZ. JOHNNIE WALKER BLACK LABEL

•

For the GBP:

200 ML/7 FL. OZ. WARM WATER

7G/¼ OZ. CHAMPAGNE YEAST

50 G/2 OZ. SUGAR

25 G/1 OZ. GROUND GINGER

•

For the GBP, Put the water, yeast, 10 g/⅓ oz. of the sugar and 5 g/⅙ oz. of the ginger into a sterilized container and stir well. Set aside in a warm place, covered. Every day for 4 days, add a further 10 g/⅓ oz. sugar and 5 g/⅙ oz. ginger. After 5 days you will have a finished GBP, which should be visibly alive and bubbling away nicely. This can then be refrigerated, or fed every few days to maintain a healthy culture.

To make the cocktail, first, sterilize a pair of 1-litre/1-quart plastic bottles. Bring a third of the water to the boil and add the chilli, fresh ginger, lemon zest and cream of tartar. Immediately remove from the heat and allow to cool for 10 minutes, stirring continuously. Pass it through a sieve/strainer, then dissolve the sugar in it. Add the rest of the water, along with the whisky. Finally, whisk in the GBP and transfer the liquid to the bottles.

Leave in a warm place for exactly 2 days, then transfer to the refrigerator for 1 day. Drink within 2 weeks. As with anything involving yeast, there's always an element of unpredictability (explosions are not unheard of), so the best practice is to store bottles far away from anything valuable.

IRISH COFFEE

60 ML/¼ CUP DOUBLE/HEAVY CREAM

150 ML/5¼ FL. OZ. ETHIOPIAN COFFEE
(such as Yirgacheffe, or something similarly floral and peachy)

35 ML/1¼ FL. OZ. GREEN SPOT IRISH WHISKEY

5 G/1 TEASPOON SUGAR

•

Put the cream in a cream whipper (or beat it by hand in a stainless-steel bowl) and warm it in bowl of hot water for 30 minutes. Brew the coffee, then add the sugar and whisky and allow to cool in the cup for 5–10 minutes. Dispense the warm cream on top and serve immediately.

Glass: Beer mug

I have long preached that Irish coffee is one of the world's biggest abominations. Indeed, even the finest Irish whiskey and most delicious coffee can do a very good job of obliterating each others' redeeming features, resulting in slightly alcoholic coffee with a peculiar, 'woody' taste to it.

Now that I've finished burying the entire concept of an Irish coffee, it's time to reveal the only recipe that I would ever use to combine the two in liquid harmony. To explain, first let's look at the origins of Irish coffee to understand the reason for its existence.

It's the famous wet winter of 1942 and consequent grounded planes at Shannon Airport in Ireland that force delayed passengers to hole up in the airport bar. Bartender Joe Sheridan observes his weary patrons and takes the unprecedented step, which eludes so many bartenders, of inventing a classic cocktail. Whether it was known to him or not, the combination of sugar, fat, alcohol and caffeine provides everything the body needs in situations that demand extreme levels of pick-me-up-ness.

The key to making a great Irish coffee is matching the coffee and whiskey sympathetically. To do this we must first find the character traits they have in common. This might be the caramel character shared by Redbreast 12-year-old and a single-origin coffee from Guatemala, for example. I also believe that lighter whiskies and coffees tend to work better, which is as good a reason as any to continue using Irish whiskey.

The second important consideration is temperature. Make the drink too hot and it becomes spirity and unpleasant, requiring more sugar to counteract the dryness of the alcohol. It must be balanced with the cream on top, which acts as a kind of insulation blanket for the lips as you sip through to the main event. I prefer to serve the cream and coffee at the same temperature. I would always recommend making the coffee in a cafetière/French press, which gives the greatest clarity in the cup and allows the flavour of the coffee to shine. Use white sugar, not brown, which will distort the flavour of the coffee and whiskey.

WHISKY GUMS

200 ML/7 FL. OZ. WHISKY (SEE BELOW)

30 G/1¼ OZ. POWDERED GELATINE

180 G/½ CUP LIQUID GLUCOSE

150 G/¾ CUP SUGAR

5 G/1 TEASPOON MALIC ACID

ICING/CONFECTIONERS' SUGAR, FOR DUSTING

•

Put half the whisky in a saucepan and heat it to at least 60°C/140°F with the gelatine, whisking until fully dissolved. Remove it from the heat and set aside. Add the remaining ingredients, except the icing/confectioners' sugar, to another pan and heat until they form a caramel, removing it from the heat only once it reaches exactly 126°C/259°F. Allow to cool to below 100°C/212°F, then quickly mix in the gelatine mixture and pour into greased chocolate moulds. Place in the fridge for a few hours, then turn out and dust with icing/confectioners' sugar.

This idea came from a visit to the Fat Duck restaurant in Bray, England. My good friend Jocky Petrie was head of the development kitchen there and I was lucky enough to spend a day working with him in 2010. One of the innovative courses aimed to recreate the classic wine-gum candy, only this time it had real booze in it and it was whisky!

The Fat Duck made four different 'whisky gums', each from a different single malt, and I found it an excellent way to appreciate the differences in flavour without having to sip my way through four glasses. Also, the fact that the alcohol was evaporated off and tempered by some sweetness meant that some flavours were made more apparent than they would normally be. The flip side was that the drop in alcohol also dumbed down some of the more complex spice, tannin and dry fruitiness you might expect to get from a good glass of whisky. I think there's also something to be said

for the mouthfeel and thick texture in this recipe; when coupled with the usual whisky characteristics, it highlights a sort of primal, nectar-like quality that I think is present in all malt spirits, but usually only as a distant backdrop.

The Fat Duck's recipe for these gums makes a melt-in-the-mouth jelly that softens when it hits the palate, then lingers, getting more gloopy as it melts. However, I wanted my gums to be more reminiscent of the jaw-achingly chewy gums sold in twisted plastic packets when I was young. I've also included a couple of ingredients that give that mouth-puckering sweet-and-sour effect.

The whisky is up to you, but I recommend making a selection of gums that cover a broad spectrum of flavour. Stand-out gums for me have been Lagavulin 16-year-old, Highland Park 18-year-old, Glenfarclas 15-year-old, Jameson Irish Whiskey, Four Roses Yellow Label and Jack Daniel's Gentleman Jack.

HET PINT & COG

200 ML/7 FL. OZ. HIGHLAND PARK 12-YEAR-OLD

50 ML/2 FL. OZ. SWEET OLOROSO SHERRY

400 ML/14 FL. OZ. SINCLAIR BREWERIES RED MACGREGOR ALE

100 G/½ OZ. CASTER/SUPERFINE SUGAR

3 ALLSPICE BERRIES, 3 CLOVES AND 1 LARGE CINNAMON STICK

•

Put all the ingredients in a saucepan, cover with a lid and heat gently. Monitor the temperature using a thermometer, and once the mixture reaches 75°C/167°F, scoop out and discard the spices and serve. You can use other beers, but Sinclair Breweries Red MacGregor from Orkney is the real deal and the only true Orcadian way to make a Cog. Serves 6

When I visited the island of Orkney and the Highland Park Distillery, my good friend Daryl Haldane let me in on a little Orkney tradition of drinking whisky from a cog. I'd never heard of this ritual before. Further research revealed that no one outside of Orkney had ever come across it, let alone written about it. For that reason, I believe this to be the first and only whisky book to include a cog recipe.

The cog itself looks like an ornate bucket, and is very similar in style to a classic Viking bucket. No surprises there, given the level of Scandinavian influence on the island. The bucket is distinguishable by two, sometimes three, vertical handles that follow the angle of the bowl. Usually cogs are large, capable of holding around two or three litres of liquid, but smaller ones (like the one pictured) are also available. It's possible that the cog is named after the cog boat from the 10th century, since the bucket is somewhat reminiscent of the protruding bow and stern.

It's customary to serve a cog at weddings on Orkney, where it acts like a kind of shared punchbowl. Traditionally,

there are three cogs that circulate around the room, the geud (best) man's, the priest's and the bride's. When the cog is passed on, the guest grips the handles and quaffs a mouthful of punch, then passes it on to the next guest. The three-handled versions are rare and were apparently created so that the bride's father could grip the spare handle and prevent over-eager guests from sampling more than they were due!

The drink that goes into the cog is reminiscent of some old Scandinavian beverages, but the fact that it contains whisky tells us that there's no small amount of Scottish influence here, too. The drink is very similar to the classic het pint, which is traditionally drunk during the Scottish Hogmanay (New Year). Where they differ is that cog doesn't normally have egg in it, unlike the het pint, which is more of a beer and whisky eggnog. Cog recipes vary across Orkney, and some families have a proprietary formula that they guard with their lives. This recipe is based on a combination of some of the recipes that I overheard in Orkney, with a few extra flourishes.

MIZUWARI

50 ML/2 FL. OZ. NIKKA FROM THE BARREL
150 ML/5¼ FL. OZ. SCOTTISH MINERAL WATER (OR WATER OF YOUR CHOICE)

•

Put a few chunks of hand-cracked ice in a highball glass; if you can get hold of the crystal-clear stuff, then all the better. Add the whisky and water and stir for 1 minute. Japanese tradition dictates that you should stir only 3½ times, but I feel it benefits from a little extra chilling. Try not to disrupt the ice too much; it should be a quiet process. Remove the spoon and serve with a warm oshibori (towel).

Glass: Highball tumbler

The Japanese ritual of *mizuwari* is a great example of the simplicity of whisky winning through. On the face of it, this drink is nothing more than whisky, water and ice, but if there's one thing that the Japanese do well, it's ice. If there's another thing they do well, it's whisky. And they're not bad at water, either.

I was intrigued the first time I was served a Mizuwari by legendary bartender Kichi-San in Tokyo's underground Star Bar. Suntory Yamazaki, hand-cracked ice and crystal-clear water were added to a glass, and the concoction was silently and skilfully stirred for just the right length of time. A quick sniff alerted me to some faint aromatics of whisky, but it was in the taste where I was really surprised. The liquid itself was very cold indeed, and whipped around my mouth with tropical fruits like pineapple and lychee, then slipped away like a fruity little serpent. The other surprising thing was the sweetness – oh, the sweetness! – despite having had no sugar added at all. I put much of that down to the gloopiness of the liquid post-chilling. Since then I've often heavily diluted whisky to see what effect it has on the flavour. Take it (almost) out of the equation, and you

have the opportunity to experience whisky in a whole new light.

Bourbon & Branch is a similar drink traditionally drunk in America. I was first introduced to it by the Ian Fleming novel *Diamonds Are Forever*, in which Bond orders one because it is 'fashionable in racing circuits'. The author goes on to explain that 'real bourbon drinkers insist on having their whiskey in the traditional style, with water from high up in the branch of the local river where it will be purest'. It seems that whisky-drinkers in the 1960s were a discerning crowd.

I've seen many a distiller and blender brooding over the effect that different types of water have on whiskies. Once water becomes 75% of your drink, things like the pH, mineral content and TDS (total dissolved solids) begin to have a big impact on flavour perception. Mineral salts are very much like table salt, and so can accentuate certain characteristics as well as providing a harder, more chalky texture. Soft water, with a lower TDS, tends to feel sweeter as it slinks around your mouth, and water with a high (alkaline) or low (acid) pH can give a boost to spicy flavours and smoke.

HOT TODDY

500 ML/17½ FL. OZ. THE BALVENIE DOUBLEWOOD

100 G/3½ OZ. HONEY

100 G/½ CUP SUGAR

150 ML/5¼ FL. OZ. FRESHLY SQUEEZED LEMON JUICE

3 LARGE CINNAMON STICKS, 5 WHOLE CLOVES, 1 STAR ANISE AND 5 SPRIGS OF LAVENDER

LEMON SLICES, TO GARNISH

•

Put all the ingredients in a sealable bottle and give it a good shake. Allow to sit for a good week before using. To prepare the drink, pour 60 ml/¼ cup Toddy Infusion into a mug and top up with 150 ml/⅔ cup hot water. Garnish with a slice of lemon.

Take a quick flick through the history pages of this book and you will find references to the medicinal uses of whisky. There's a reason that they call it 'Grandpa's old cough medicine': only 80 years ago it would have been possible, in the US, to get a prescription from a doctor for medicated whiskey. These days we are aware of the negative impact that alcohol can have on our health, but for short-term gains, whisky should not be underestimated.

In fact, as I write this very line I regret to inform you, dear reader, that I have been overcome with a bout of the common cold. Needless to say, I have taken measures to relieve my condition by way of carefully (self-) prescribed whisky. I am pleased to report that it has lifted my mood and settled my ailments.

The hot toddy is not the only antidotal whisky-based drink out there – whisky on its own does a pretty good job – but it is perhaps the best of them. Thought to be named after the Indian drink 'toddy', made from fermented palm sap, the Hot Toddy is a veritable dream-team of medicinal heavyweights. Hell, I don't think I've ever drunk one when I didn't have an illness of some sort!

There's an old Scottish cold remedy that instructs the patient to retire to bed with a large whisky toddy, to hang a bowler hat at the foot of the bed, and drink until there appear to be two hats. Obviously the chief ingredient here is whisky, and the alcohol contained within is a one-two punch of antiseptic and anaesthetic. Next is the lemon, full of vitamin C (and also an antiseptic) and sour, to refresh the mouth. Then there's sugar and honey, which balance the lemon, but more importantly, provides instant-access energy. Spices augment the ensemble though anaesthetic effect (cloves) and heated invigoration (cinnamon). Lastly, there's hot water, which extracts and interacts with all the other ingredients, then vaporizes them to form hot steam that cleanses the olfactory system and soothes the throat.

My recipe sticks to the basic toddy formula, but I've included a few additional ingredients and tweaked others.

First, let me tell you that I am not the greatest advocate of off-the-shelf cream liqueurs. It's not so much to do with the flavour – I actually quite like the taste of Baileys and its close relatives – it's more to do with the audacity of the whole thing, that someone, at some point, deemed it OK to combine Irish whiskey and fresh cream in a shelf-stable bottle. God knows what sordid procedures the manufacturers of these products have developed to make the stuff last so long. Deals have been made with the devil, though, and even an open bottle is guaranteed by the manufacturer to taste good for at least two years. If the nukes hit tomorrow, the surviving cockroaches could live off Baileys.

The stability of the product is helped along by the alcohol content, which stops the cream from souring, but there is also a complex series of homogenization (refining particle size) and emulsification (preventing separation of fats) processes that depend on added emulsifiers and vegetable oil, among other things. So it struck me that it would be nice to make an Irish cream liqueur that forgoes the shelf life, but tastes delicious while it lasts.

The first Irish cream liqueur was Baileys, which was launched in 1974. Its origins can be found in such drinks as the 'flip' (eggs, sugar, spirit, spice) and of course in Irish coffee (see page 136). In a sense, it is a cold Irish coffee that has been stirred together to form a kind of a coherent, milky mass. The difference with the liqueur is that it must be composed of at least 40% Irish whiskey – by my reckoning – to achieve the necessary

IRISH CREAM LIQUEUR

800 ML/3½ CUPS WHOLE MILK

0.5 G VANILLA SEEDS

25 G/1 OZ. CACAO NIBS

200 G/1 CUP SUGAR

5 G/1 TEASPOON SALT

15 G/½ OZ. FRESHLY COARSE-GROUND COFFEE

400 ML/1¾ CUPS BUSHMILLS BLACK BUSH

150 ML/⅔ CUP DOUBLE/HEAVY CREAM

1–2 G SODIUM ALGINATE (OPTIONAL)

•

Sterilize a suitable bottle to hold your liqueur, either by boiling it in hot water or using a sterilizing solution.

Put the milk, vanilla and cacao nibs in a pan and bring to a simmer. Hold it there for 30 minutes, then strain through muslin/cheesecloth. Return the liquid to the pan along with the sugar and salt, and allow to reduce slowly for an hour, or until you are left with half the liquid – about 450 ml/2 cups in total. Turn off the heat and allow to cool for a minute, then add the coffee. Stir well and after 5 minutes, strain the liquid through a fine sieve or tea strainer Allow to cool down, then stir in the whiskey.

Put the mixture in a jug blender (or use a jug/pitcher and an immersion blender) and blitz for 20 seconds while steadily pouring in the cream. Stop the blender and pour the finished liqueur into the sterilized bottle. Keep refrigerated for up to a month. If you want to make the liqueur thicker, try adding 1–2g sodium alginate during the blending stage. It's a natural thickener of dairy products that gives the impression of a more fatty consistency without actually increasing the fat.

It keeps for at least a week in the fridge – any longer and you're not doing it right! You can serve it over ice, mix it into your cappuccino, or pour it over your dessert.

Makes approximately 1 litre/4¼ cups

alcoholic strength. If the strength of the liqueur is below 16%, it is at a greater risk of spoiling quickly.

My recipe includes a selection of spices and flavourings, too, which both enhance and balance some of the flavours present in the cream and the whiskey. The quantities of these ingredients are my own recommendations, and you can adjust them if you want to knock back or lift up a specific flavour.

Amylase Malting enzyme that converts starch into its soluble form; also found in saliva.

Bære Oldest variety of British barley.

Backset *see* sour mash.

Beta-glucan Starch family prevalent in rye grain; partly responsible for its gluey consistency when mashed.

Bourbon cask 180–200-litre (90–211-quart) charred American oak cask.

Bushel Old unit of measurement equivalent to eight gallons and used commonly for cereals.

Butt Large 500-litre (528-quart) cask traditionally used for storing Sherry.

Caramel Non-sweet colour additive used to add the effect of longer maturation and for colour consistency. Not permitted in bourbon and straight whiskey.

Charring Non-penetrative and aggressive flame burning of the internal surface of a cask to liberate flavourful compounds and aid with spirit interaction; barrels may be charred to various degrees.

Chill filtering Controversial finishing process used for some whiskies wherein the liquid is cooled to below 0°C (32°F) and filtered to remove flavourless residual haze that can be unsightly. Critics believe the process also removes body and flavour.

Cooper/cooperage Maker/raiser of barrels for the wine and spirits industry.

Diastase Malting enzymes that are naturally present within cereals.

Doubler Pot still used in the distillation of American whiskey through which the alcohol from the continuous still passes to create the final spirit.

Draff Spent cereals left over after mashing. High in fibre and protein, these are processed into animal feed.

Drum malting Think tumble/spin dryer that turns and cools barley grains during malting.

Ester A chemical compound formed by the interaction of an acid and an alcohol; typically smells fruity and floral.

Feints The last alcohol to come through on the final (typically second) distillation. Low in alcohol and high in fusel oils, these are mixed with foreshots and redistilled in the next spirit run.

First-fill A barrel that is being filled for the first time with malt whisky/Irish whiskey, but has typically already been filled with bourbon or Sherry – so actually it is a second fill!

Foreshots The first spirit to emerge during the final (typically second) distillation. High in alcohol and some dangerous volatiles, these are redistilled with the feints in the next spirit run.

Floor malting Traditional process of malting barley, where the grains are spread evenly across a large floor space and regularly turned over, typically over a week-long period (but it varies).

Germination Hormonal trigger that kicks-off growth mechanisms in barley during malting.

Gramineae Family of grasses to which all major cereals belong.

Green malt Malted barley before it has been dried.

Hogshead 250-litre (264-quart) cask made from American oak, usually by adding extra staves into a bourbon cask.

Kiln drying Process of halting the germination and malting process though heating with or without peat.

Lauter Filtering screen in the base of a mash tun.

Lyne arm The elbow at the top of a pot still that carries alcohol vapour from the body of the still to the condenser. Lyne-arm angle and gauge affects the character of the spirit.

Malting Process of enzyme-based cell-wall destruction, typically in barley.

Mothballed A distillery that has ceased production, but not been decommissioned.

Peat Plant matter that has decomposed over thousands of years in an acidic environment with poor drainage. When cut, dried and burned, it is a crude fuel source, traditionally used to dry malted barley, which imparts a smokiness into the finished whisky.

Phenol/Phenolic Organic compounds derived from peat reek that imparts tarry, smoky, charred and burnt characteristics to a whisky.

PPM Phenolic parts per million. The industry-standard measurement for smokiness in peat-dried barley. A 10ppm malt sample contains 10 phenolic parts for every 999,990 non-phenolic parts. PPM is almost always a measurement of malt phenolics, not the phenolic part of a finished whisky, which is usually much less.

Reek The phenolic smoke produced by burning peat.

Reflux The (repeated) condensing of vapours within a still before it has reached the condenser proper. Reflux is controlled by temperature and time and is one way of producing a lighter spirit.

Rummager Turning chain in a still that helps to prevent build-up of residue on the inside of the base.

Saladin box Large-scale malting that takes place in cooled troughs and turned by a large corkscrew.

Seasoning Practice of filling a new-oak cask with spirit or wine (bourbon, Sherry, Madeira etc.) prior to actual maturation of the product to extract 'new wood' influence over the spirit.

Shiel Shovel-like tool used to turn barley grains when floor malting.

Solera From the Spanish word meaning 'ground', or 'earth'. This is a system of cask maturation whereby casks are filled in tiers from top to bottom with the lower tiers being filled from the upper. Spirit is only removed from the bottom tier, hence the name solera. Each tier is never completely emptied, meaning that some small amount of whisky will remain in the system throughout the lifespan of the system, aiding in consistency and in a way doing the job of a whisky blender.

Sour mash American whiskey process of adding the sour leftovers from the previous distillation into the fermenter along with the next mash. This lowers the pH and promotes good fermentation.

Sparge Wetting cereals in a mash tun to extract fermentable sugars.

Stave Shaped piece of wood used to construct a cask.

Tannin Coloured substance extracted from wood that gives a sensation like a drying bitterness on the tongue. Derivative of gallic acid.

Thumper A doubler containing water, which helps to remove some heavier alcohols and 'cleans' the spirit a little bit.

Toasting Penetrative heating of the internal surfaces of a barrel to liberate flavourful compounds and aid spirit interaction; barrels may be toasted to a variety of different degrees.

Volatile Molecules with evaporative tendencies that distil easily and, assuming they are not odourless, can also be smelled easily.

Wash Alcoholic beer produced from the fermentation of wort; in the US it is referred to simply as 'beer'.

Worm tub Traditional manner of converting alcohol vapour into liquid. A 'worm' is a coiled pipe that sits in a 'tub' of cool water, as the vapour passes through the coil it condenses into new-make spirit. Worm tubs typically give a heavier, more sulphurous spirit.

Wort Sugar-rich liquid drawn from the cooking of cereal grains in a mash tun.

SCOTLAND

ISLAY

Ardbeg The darling of Islay and favourite of the International Space Station. Ardbeg is characterized by lots of peat and light body. Uiegaidail is a particularly good release from this distillery.

Bowmore A pioneer in every sense, Bowmore is one of the oldest Scotch distilleries, and was one of the first to achieve cult status in the 1990s. The distillery still has an active maltings floor and the location is nothing short of breathtaking. I highly recommend old Bowmore from the 1970s.

Bruichladdich Bought by drinks giant Rémy Cointreau and formerly Ian McEwan as production director (one of the greatest talents in the Scotch whisky industry), this distillery is operated largely by Victorian-era equipment. Its warehouses contain a huge spectrum of timber, coming from Sherry industries, bourbon and first-growth bordeaux.

Caol Ila In the past, most of the spirit made here at this Diageo-owned distillery was used in blends like Johnnie Walker, and much of it still is. But Caol Ila or 'Sound of Islay' has emerged as a competitive standalone malt in recent years, and rightly so, as some of the special releases have been mind-blowing.

Bunnahabhain Perched on the north-east coast in the picturesque village of Bunnhabhain (founded in 1881 to house the distillery's workers), this distillery was notable as it produced no peated whisky whatsoever, a highly unusual situation for Islay. Things changed in 2004 with the release of 6-year-old Moine (Gaelic for 'peat') in response to the increased demand in the late 1990s and early 2000s.

Kilchoman One of the younger distilleries on Islay, Kilchoman's more mature expressions now show us how the zesty, mineral whiskies it does so well have developed in oak.

Lagavulin Records of 'The Mill in the Valley' go back as far as the mid-1700s. This, the other Diageo-owned distillery on Islay, produces much less whisky than its big, friendly brother Caol Ila, however the quality of the liquid is prized so much that a far larger proportion finds its way into official bottlings than to blends.

Laphroaig The crown prince of peat. Almost half of all the whisky bottled and sold as malt from Islay has a Laphroaig label on it, with the 10-year-old and Quarter Cask both being very popular expressions. Like Bowmore, Laphroaig still operates a floor malting.

SPEYSIDE

Aberlour France's most popular malt, Aberlour has achieved more than any other mid-century Speyside distillery. Why? Well, it would have to be its herbal, fruity and green character – ideal for blenders and as a stand-alone malt, especially when mixed with Sherry wood.

Alt-a-Bhainne Major contributor to the Chivas blend, but available as a malt bottling under the 'Deerstalker' brand.

Ardmore A big contributor to the Teacher's blend, owned by Beam Inc. Ardmore was the last Scottish distillery to abandon direct coal-firing in 2002, so look out for older independent bottles. Unusually for Speyside this dram tends to be slightly peated.

Auchroisk Pronounced *au-thrusk*. Big distillery and under-represented Speyside dram that contributes to Diageo blends. Has a unique clingy mouthfeel and cheesecake qualities.

Aultmore Looks like a school, tastes like a sweet/candy shop. Big contributor to Dewar's blends, but has been available in a 12-year-old bottling since 2004.

Balmenach Former family-owned distillery of Sir Robert Bruce Lockhart, now run by Inver House and also used to produce Caorunn gin. Almost everything made here finds its way in to the Hankey Bannister blend. Sulphury new make.

Balvenie The smaller sibling to Glenfiddich and producer of the ever-popular Doublewood bottlings. Still run by David Stewart, the longest-serving distiller in Scotland (52 years!). Balvenie is the great absorber of wood.

The BenRiach Founded in 1898, this troubled distillery has mainly played supporting roles such as supplying malt to its older brother Longmorn. Today the majority of its alcohol now goes into the Chivas Blend, where once more it encounters Longhorn, but I expect to see good things from them in the future.

Benrinnes Another Diageo-owned hidden gem, being as close as you're likely to get to Mortlach for sheer meaty nutrition, which is probably at least partly down to a proprietary distillation process. Some excellent Independent bottles available from Master of Malt.

Benromach Speyside's quaint, small-scale distillery was the first ever to produce a whisky certified as 100% organic by the Soil Association. Benromach Organic is matured exclusively in Virgin Oak Barrels.

Braeval Located in the Braes (high valley) of Glenlivet, this distillery was formerly known as the Brae O' Glenlivet. It's the same elevation as Dalwhinnie at 355 m/1,165 ft. and adheres to the contemporary Speyside style.

Cardhu One of the only active distilleries in Scotland that was founded by a woman, Cardhu is now run by Diageo and makes up an important part of the Johnnie Walker blended whiskies as well as producing its own core range.

Cragganmore Founded in 1870 by John Smith, of The Macallan, The Glenlivet and Glenfarclas fame. Unusually, the stills here have flat tops and use traditional worm-tub condensers. A very decent dram.

Craigellachie This big Dewar's contributor shares the town of Craigellachie with the better-known The Macallan Distillery, as well as the famous Craigellachie Hotel, which sports one of the best whisky bars in the world.

Dailuaine The first distillery to be fitted with a pagoda roof, back in 1889, Dailuaine is honeyed, grassy and fruity. Over 98% of Dailuaine's 3.4 million litres (3.6 million quarts) a year of alcohol goes into Diageo's blends. Pretty good stuff.

Dufftown Besides being the chief fellow in Diageo's Singleton label whisky, Dufftown is also an environmentally sound distillery. All but 3% of their product goes into blends.

Glenallachie Rarely bottled as a malt, this distillery, opened in 1967, is owned by Pernod Ricard and contributes virtually all of its product to the Chivas blends. Gloriously unexceptional.

Glenburgie Grassy, agricultural and silage are words that describe Glenburgie. As unappealing as that might sound, this distillery does manage to secure some individuality in a section of Speyside that is guilty of slipping into blind mundanity.

Glendullan Dull by name... dull by nature. In the past, Glendullan has been bottled under Diageo's 'Singleton' label, but for the most part this is a blend filler, fruity and green.

Glen Elgin The glint in the blender's eye, Glen Elgin now enjoys pride of place within Diageo's Classic Malt range.

Glenfarclas The first distillery to launch a cask-strength whisky in 1968, this family-owned, 150-year-old business has a highly unusual wood policy (they reuse ex-Sherry casks up to four times) that puts a firm stamp on their spirit – expect to find tobacco, fruit cake and vibrant florals throughout the range.

Glenfiddich In 1963 Glenfiddich became the first distillery to release and market a single malt whisky in the UK and in 2011 reached the landmark sales figure of 1 million nine-litre/quart cases in a year. This, the best-known malt whisky in the world, is in danger of becoming an overlooked back-bar staple (being as approachably malty and citrussy as it is tame) and here to stay. But it has been supplemented with some fantastic older expressions and special releases.

Glen Grant Light, thanks to nice, tall stills and purifiers. Glen Grant used to describe its whisky as 'pale with a colourful past'; colour is added liberally these days, however. But it's still one of the cleanest new-make whiskies in Scotland today.

The Glenlivet A distillery that has earned its place in history, the Glenlivet is truly the benchmark for Scotch malt. The second-biggest malt whisky distillery in Scotland, it produces the most popular Scotch in the USA bar none. Floral and orchard fruits define the distillery.

Glenlossie Diageo's Glenlossie Distillery stores over 200,000 casks – big by Scottish standards. The tropical-tasting whisky itself is rare, however, and usually only available as a Flora & Fauna bottling.

Glen Moray Located in the heart of Elgin (and surrounded by a housing estate) the whisky from Glen Moray tends to be about as exciting as its location suggests.

Glenrothes Like Balblair, Glenrothes is another flag-flyer of vintages over age statements. The distillery is owned by Edrington, but all official bottlings come from Berry Bros.

Glen Spey A feeder for the J&B blend, very little Glen Spey sees daylight through a bottle that isn't green. Expect nutty, greasy, bourbon-like characteristics.

Glentauchers Founded by blender James Buchanan, in 1889. Exceptional only for its unnatural and unsuccessful experiments with continuous distillation of malt whisky in the early 20th century.

Inchgower Diageo-owned distillery and a harlot of the blending world, being used for both its owner's stock as well as selling out to rival firms. Tasty, though, and unique in that it was collectively owned by the town of Buckie in the 1930s.

Kininvie Lesser-known runt of the William Grant litter (Glenfiddich, Balvenie) Kininvie is an unabashed blend jockey, but not a bad dram in its own right... if you can track a bottle down. Dufftown, Banffshire.

Knockando Run of the mill at best. It was the first distillery in Speyside to have electricity, however... that's about it.

Knockdhu Also known as anCnoc (Gaelic for 'the hill'). This distillery changed its name in 2001 after Inverhouse bought it. Still a good dram.

Linkwood An under-represented dram if ever there was one. Linkwood is a massively subtle, complex and fragrant dram, with a great weighty mouthfeel. I expect to see more in the future.

Longmorn Highly prized single malt with a dedicated fanbase, despite the vast majority ending up in one of Pernod Ricards blended whiskies. Even a small amount of this awesome malt will add a flourish to any blend, which is still the biggest category of whisky sold globally.

The Macallan The Sherry-cask whiskies generate a good deal of hype among those with deep pockets. Unusually, The Macallan is labelled as a highland malt, despite being right in the middle of Speyside.

Mannochmore Yet another phantom Diageo distillery, which proves more useful as a cask stash than it does as a producer of anything especially noteworthy. That's not to say it's bad, however; expect to find delicate spice and good flavour clarity.

Miltonduff Not to be confused with the Milton (Strathisla) Distillery (which is also owned by Chivas) or Macduff Distillery (owned by Dewar's). Miltonduff has a peppered history, having once conducted a triple distillation and at another time owning a pair of Lomond stills, which were used to produce a malt called Misstowie. One to watch.

Mortlach Diageo-owned and with 90–95% of its production destined for a Johnnie Walker, prized for the hearty backbone it provides. Much of its character is put down to its unique

'2.81x' distillation process, along with the 100% use of cold worm tubs that helps to reduce copper contact.

Roseisle Opened in 2009, this is the most technologically advanced malt distillery in Scotland today. Affectionately referred to as The Death Star, it was purpose-designed and engineered to produce multiple styles of whisky all under the same roof, and with a zero carbon footprint to boot. They are attempting to re-write the malt whisky rulebook, but perhaps the most desirable malt whisky traits will forever remain beyond the understanding of science and engineering... time will tell.

Speyburn An underachiever, this one. Creating a fruity and well-bodied style, partly thanks to the worm tub, this distillery was the first (in 1897) to have a drum malting on site – in a time where everyone else was still raking floors.

Speyside Ironically, this distillery in Glen Tromie, which only began production in 1990, is barely within the walls of the Speyside region, being stuck right out on the south-western border. Unfortunately, it's not a stand-out dram, either.

Strathisla Oldest operating distillery in the Highlands, dating back to 1786. Most goes to Chivas blends. The 12-year-old release is all about pickled walnuts and Chardonnay.

Strathmill Another Diageo blend-donkey. You can find a 12-year-old Flora and Fauna release, it's clean, dry and nutty.

Tamdhu Large-scale, but unremarkable distillery, recently brought back from the dead by Ian Macleod Distillers in 2012. Tamdhu was the last distillery to conduct malting in Saladin boxes.

Tamnavulin Light and malty, just like its 1960s brethren, Tomintoul and Tormore (below), Tamnavulin is innocuous almost to the point of cowardice.

Tomintoul With the self-prescribed sub-heading of 'the gentle dram' you might expect this to sit alongside light Speyside representatives, but Tomintoul also produces a heavily peated variation, which is smoked using locally sourced peat.

Tormore Designed by Sir Albert Richardson, Tormore is perhaps my favourite-looking distillery in Scotland. It dates back to 1960, which makes it the first truly new-built distillery in Scotland in the 20th century. It looks like an art deco fortress and is hard to miss if you're driving through Speyside on the A96. Lightly peated, agreeable expressions.

HIGHLANDS

Aberfeldy Core malt of the Dewar's blends, which has seen little limelight itself up until recently. That's about to change, however, so keep an eye out for this nutty, apple-y, honeyed malt.

Ardmore Teacher's pet (blend monkey). Heavily peated, yet delicately aromatic, Ardmore is one of Scotland's largest distilleries and still has its own cooperage, which is used for cask repairs. Stills were coal-fired until 2001, so I wouldn't be surprised to see a subtle change in recent younger expressions.

Balblair Part of the coastal Highland cluster that also contains the likes of Glenmorangie, Clynelish and The Dalmore, poor Balblair is a victim of overshadowing by big, noisy neighbours. It is, however, a family operation and one of the oldest active distilleries in Scotland. Its unique and carefully streamlined range and progressive way of packaging its products, are just two of the many things that make it a hidden gem in my opinion.

Ben Nevis As the name suggests, this distillery sits at the foot of the most famous 'Ben' in Britain. It has experienced its fair share of weirdness over the years, and for 3 decades it produced both malt and grain whisky side by side. It closed in the mid-80s but in 1989 saviours came in the form of the Japanese giant Nikka. Quality has improved since then, but it's still all about sticking to traditional practices for Ben Nevis, and it remains the only distillery in Scotland that uses only Brewer's yeast for fermentation.

Blair Athol The home of the Bell's blend. An easy distillery visit from either Edinburgh or Glasgow. While you're there be sure to pick up a bottle of the distillery-only cask-strength first-fill Sherry bottling.

Clynelish This distillery exists on the site of the Brora distillery, which was formerly known as Clynelish. It's complicated basically... But, it is here in the coastal village of Brora or 'Electric City' as it is nicknamed locally, that we find one of my favourite whiskies in the world. This honeyed, lustrous and infamously 'waxy' whisky offers a unique experience to malt drinkers, and is a great friend of the blenders too.

The Dalmore Sought-after all over the world, The Dalmore is a powerful whisky, capable of holding its own through extended periods of time in European oak casks. Old Dalmore can be especially complex stuff, like stuffing a cigar box filled with fruit cake and liqueur chocolates in your mouth all at once. Whyte & Mackay have owned the brand since 1960 and taken full advantage of these superpowers with a vast array of special release bottles (on top of the core expressions) that have found their place within the realms of high-rollers who place at least as much emphasis on the status that a bottle affords them as they do the flavour of the liquid inside.

Dalwhinnie The meeting place. Possibly Scotland's most gazed-upon distillery, positioned only a few hundred metres off the western side of the A9. Joint highest in Scotland (with Braeval). Sat between the Cairngorm and the Monadhliath ranges, it is isolated, cold and very tasty. Chocolate, honey, orange.

Deanston Another surprising distillery. Deanston generates all its electricity requirements (and then some) from turbines in the River Teith. The whisky is good, too: docile, warm and a little waxy.

Edradour 'Scotland's smallest distillery', The Edradour in Pitlochry, has the feel of a model village about it. A whisky-making operation was founded on this site in around 1825 and the first mention of Edradour came about 10 years later. The distillery makes two different whiskies, unpeated Edradour and heavily peated Ballechin. First-fill Sherry and bourbon casks are a standard of living which Edradour has become accustomed to...

Fettercairn A distillery that's seen its fair share of ownership over the years. There's been some interesting kit here, too: soap grinders on the side of the stills (to reduce frothing), stainless-steel condensers (replaced with copper in 1995) and a kind of cold-water cooling system that runs down the side of the stills. A weird one.

Glencadam The long-closed distillery was bought by Angus Dundee in 2003 and production is now set at 24 hours a day, seven days a week. A good chunk of Glencadam's capacity still fills the blender's bottle, but as a standalone malt I believe it to be a hidden gem. Blending it is, in this author's humble opinion, like putting sashimi grade sushi in a fish pie. With vulnerability, poise, a slight salinity and crisp florals, it might be one of the most underrated whiskies in Scotland.

Glendronach A whisky that loves ex-Sherry casks and that has the muscle to keep them at bay. Old expressions are fantastic. Recent investment in 2009 means we can probably expect to see some new additions to the range soon.

Glen Garioch Scotland's first gas-fired distillery (in 1982) produces a powerful, rich dram that does well over long periods of maturation. At 25,000 litres (26,500 quarts) it also has one of the biggest wash stills in Scotland.

Glengoyne You'd never know that you're only 30 minutes from the centre of Glasgow in this picturesque distillery, complete with waterfall. There's more than just a pretty setting to Glengoyne, mind you; the 17-year-old is a great dram. Pay close attention.

Glenglassaugh Despite being nearly 140 years old, this distillery has only been active for 64 of those years. It still remains to be seen what the new Dutch owner will do with it.

Glenmorangie The clue is in the name when it comes to flavour of this poster boy/girl whisky: the exceptionally tall stills afford this dram notes of orange sorbet, mango, toffee and anything else orange you care to think of.

Glen Ord Somewhat of a monster, thanks to the large Glen Ord drum maltings that provide malt for at least six of Diageo's distilleries. Glen Ord recently found brief fame under the 'Singleton' label, which was readily available in the USA for a time. Green, damp and slightly smoky.

Glenturret Built on the same site as the Hosh Distillery, which was founded in 1775 and closed in 1921, Glenturret tenuously claims to be the oldest distillery in Scotland. Popular with visitors, Glenturret is the home of The Famous Grouse 'experience'.

Loch Lomond Weird and wonderful, Loch Lomond uses eight varieties of malt and sports three different types of still (column, pot, Lomond-esque) across four sets, meaning it can output a huge variety of products. The Inchmurrin malt is one such product produced at this distillery: clean, cool and green.

Macduff Load-carrier for the William Lawson's and Dewar's blends, but nay-a malt in its own right (officially bottled as Glen Deveron). Richer and rounder than many of the other 1960s distilleries.

Oban Distillation historian Alfred Barnard called Oban the 'Charing Cross' of the Highlands, and rightly so – Oban is one of the few distilleries in Scotland that is located right in the middle of a bustling town. It's currently the only Diageo malt that is 100% bottled as malt whisky.

Old Pulteney Set up in 1826, this distillery is located on the north-east coast of Scotland in Pulteneytown, now part of Wick. The area has a rich maritime history, and most of the distillery's employees (and customers) were fishermen. The distilling apparatus here is most peculiar. In 1886, Alfred Barnard described the stills as 'of the oldest pattern known, similar to the old smugglers kettle'. Despite this, Old Pulteney is delicious, redolent of sea foam, salt-caked fruit and old waxed leather.

Royal Brackla One of two distilleries in Scotland with the prefix 'royal', this was the first to be awarded the royal warrant back in 1835. Whisky making here is a straightforward process though, and 98% of all Royal Brackla will end up in a bottle of Dewar's. It's one of many distilleries in Scotland, whose prosaic yet reliable malts are rarely sold on their own, but play important roles as blenders.

Royal Lochnagar A contender for Scotland's most beautiful distillery. Lochnagar produces a fresh and clean new-make, despite its slight stature (it's one of the smallest in Scotland). Of the 450,000 litres (457,500 quarts) of alcohol made here, some go to the Vat 69 blend.

Strathearn Claiming to be one of the first craft whisky distilleries in Scotland, Strathearn is based on a farm just an hour north of Edinburgh. Quality over quantity is the aim, and owners Tony Reeman and David Lang are taking things back to basics by using traditional techniques and equipment to produce small batches of authentic product. The output of whisky produced by their tiny stills is minuscule, the idea being that every batch is unique.

Teaninich An oily, cutting, thick, slick dram that probably deserves more attention than it gets. Think lawnmower underbelly and you're pretty much there.

Tomatin This distillery started with two stills, and by 1986 it had 23! The same year it was bought by Takara Shuzo (the first Asian company to own a Scotch distillery – not the last) to fulfil blending needs in Asia. Sweet and fragrant.

Tullibardine Converted from a former brewery, this distillery came under new management in 2003 and, since then, has been producing some decent whiskies under former Cardhu distiller John Black.

CAMPBELLTOWN

Glengyle Started in the 1860s by one of the brothers who ran Springbank Distillery, Glengyle was forced to close in the 1920s. Some 82 years later, it was purchased by the owner of Springbank, the great-great-grandnephew of Glengyle's original owner. It began hissing back into action in 2004. Their first core product is a 12-year-old lightly peated whisky aged in both bourbon and Sherry casks. The name 'Glengyle' was already in use by another distillery, therefore Glengyle is now bottled as Kilkerran, the Gaelic name for Campbeltown.

Glen Scotia Living in the shadow of its more famous Campbeltown brother, Scotia is a good example of survivalism. The whisky is really worth trying; look out for the 7-year-old peated expression.

Springbank This distillery produces three different whisky labels: Hazelburn, Springbank and Longrow. The former is unpeated, the latter heavily peated and Springbank itself lies somewhere in the middle. Founded in 1828 and run by the same family for over 200 years, much pride is taken in the unique practices and methods that have been handed down through generations. Their steadfast survival seems proof of clever decisions.

ISLANDS

Abhainn Dearg Pronounced *aveen jarek*. This 'Red River' distillery is on the Isle of Lewis and is the most westerly distillery in Scotland and the furthest from the mainland. Stills that look like they're out of a Tim Burton movie. Early releases are... interesting.

Arran The only distillery on the Isle of Arran and a relative newcomer to island distilling. Cream, spice and fruit are common descriptors of Arran malts.

Highland Park Owned by the Edrington Group, this distillery produces a multitude of expressions from its base on the Orkney Islands. The production process has two interesting features: firstly, the use of its own distinctive Orkney peated malt, and secondly, the use of casks that have been filled with Sherry for two years first. It's these procedures, coupled with an exploration of wood influence over time, that to me makes Highland Park's whisky so highly respected.

Jura This distillery has seen its fair share of closure and neglect since its birth in 1810, perhaps partly due to the very remote location. In the 1960s, new owners started producing a light and fruity unpretentious malt whisky, sought after by many blenders at the time. In recent years, Jura has branched out into creating some much more interesting releases and its future looks promising.

Scapa A very different dram to the 'other' Orkney malt. Scapa was one of the most advanced distilleries when first founded, and the first to use steam-coil-heated stills. Today Scapa is one of only a handful of distilleries to use a Lomond still.

Talisker It may sound dramatic, but there is character on the Isle of Skye that finds its way into a bottle of Talisker. Even in old expressions, there's a primordial battle between mineral and volcanic elements on one side, and aromas of the sea and wind on the other. The distillery is now a prized possession of current owner, Diageo. Unusual mechanisms are at work in the stillhouse, with a distillation through two wash stills, a U-bend in the lyne arm and a purifier aiming to emulate the practice of triple distillation that allegedly happened here until 1925.

Tobermory The only distillery on the Isle of Mull produces two malts: Tobermory (unpeated) and Ledaig (lightly peated), the latter of which is the better, in my opinion and is named after the distillery's original name.

LOWLANDS

Ailsa Bay Don't expect to see a bottle of Ailsa Bay any time soon. In a similar vein to Diageo's Roseisle Distillery, this aims to produce a variety of styles to fulfil its owner William Grant's blending needs.

Auchentoshan The setting of this distillery in a suburb of Glasgow with the thrum of overpasses overhead won't be winning any awards, but fortunately the local spirit is 'nay half-bad'. Unusually within Scotland, this whisky maker distils 100% of its product three full times. No one knows exactly when this practice started at Auchentoshan, but this, along with a highly selective middle cut of spirit, at least 80–82% ABV, creates a tasty new make with tropical fruit character that reacts in weird and wonderful ways when introduced to an oak cask.

Bladnoch Ill-fated and oft-overlooked Lowland producer with a capacity of just 250,000 litres (264,000 quarts) per year. Bladnoch has had at least 10 owners over its 200-year-existence, and is up for sale again as we go to print.

Daftmill Tiny newcomer that produces 20,000 litres (21,000 quarts) promises to be a classic of the future. The owners are in no rush to release anything, it seems, despite their 10-year-old stocks in the warehouses now. Keep your eyes peeled.

Glenkinchie Set in gently undulating farmland 30 minutes from Edinburgh, this distillery is worth a visit for the views and for its visitor's museum with a working model of a distillery. It houses a gigantic wash still, the use of which leads to a lighter, more Lowland-y spirit, which is tempered by the use of worm tubs containing an unusual rectangular coil. A small proportion of Glenkinchie's single malt is bottled and sold each year, and the rest is used in Diageo's many blends.

The USA

There are a lot of new distilleries in the USA and quite a few have a whiskey product on their books. Many more are working on a rye, corn, malt, wheat or bourbon, and releasing vodkas, gins or liqueurs in the meantime. This glossary is a fairly comprehensive list of the distilleries that have a whiskey available to buy in 2014, but it is by no means exhaustive. I am sure to have missed a few and for that I apologize.

ARIZONA

Arizona Distilling Company Currently making malt whiskey from a mash brewed by the local Four Peaks Brewery, this distillery is also readying a durum wheat whiskey, as well as bottling its Copper City Bourbon distilled in Las Vegas.

Hamilton Distillers Producer of Del Bac Whiskey. Barley is malted in-house and dried with mesquite smoke. There are also unaged and unsmoked variants.

Thumb Butte Distillery First legal distillery in Prescott's own 'whiskey row' since Prohibition. Working on 1888 Rodeo Rye, Bloody Basin Bourbon and Central Highlands Single Malt.

ARKANSAS

Rock Town Distillery First legal distillery in Arkansas since Prohibition. This distillery makes wheated bourbon, a hickory-smoked wheat whiskey, a rye and a corn whiskey, and is working on a four-grain bourbon. Corn and wheat are both sourced from local farmers.

CALIFORNIA

American Craft Whiskey Distillers A distillery using Germain-Robin's Cognac stills to make Low Gap Whiskeys, including a 2-year-old wheat whiskey.

Anchor Distillers Of brewery fame, these guys turned their attention to distilling in 1993. Their Old Potrero Single Malt Rye has been joined by a straight rye and a single malt aged for 11 years.

Ballast Point Spirits This brewery and microdistillery makes Devil's Share Whiskey, a malt whiskey and Devil's Share Bourbon, both of which are aged in heavily charred American oak casks.

Charbay From the wine-growing region of Napa County, this distillery, celebrating its 30th year has put out two releases of its barley-based, hop-flavoured whiskey, as well as Charbay Double and Twisted Light Whiskey.

Lost Spirits Distillery This distillery makes peated single malt whiskies under the labels Seascape, Leviathan (aged in botrytized Sémillon wine casks) and Ouroboros, which is made from Californian barley, smoked with Californian peat, and matured in charred ex-Sherry Hungarian oak casks... unusual.

St. George Dubbed America's first 'craft distillery', the entire operation here is housed in an aircraft hangar. They bottle a bourbon whiskey called 'Breaking and Entering', but it's the malt whiskey they produce here that excites me. It's a blend of three 14-year-old whiskies labelled according to release number. Some of the malt used is smoked over alder and beech woods, giving it a chocolatey, nutty taste.

COLORADO

Leopold Bros. A whole host of products are made at this distillery, but they include a corn-based American whiskey, a rye and a number of flavoured whiskies made from new-make spirit.

Peachstreet Distillers Producer of various fruit- and plant-based products, including Colorado straight bourbon, which is made from locally grown corn.

Stranahan's First distilled in a horse stable Stranahan's has now filled over 5,000 casks with malt whiskey, which are being released in batch numbers. The bottle has an elongated cap, making it look rather like an alien.

Wood's High Mountain Distillery This distillery makes Tenderfoot malt whiskey, which contains a small amount of malted rye and wheat in its mash bill.

ILLINOIS

Blaum Bros. Distilling Co. This distillery makes its own bourbon, rye, wheat and malt whiskey. They have also released some sourced whiskies, including Lead Mine Moonshine, distilled by Flagler Spirits, and Knotter (i.e. 'not our') Bourbon and Rye, distilled by MGP. One to watch, on account of one of the brothers having a substantial beard.

FEW Spirits This well-thought-of distillery in the Chicago suburbs is named for the initials of Frances Elizabeth

Willard, the lady who championed the Temperance movement with the Women's Christian Temperance Union. They make very nice bourbon, malt and rye whiskies.

Koval Distillery Producer of a range of different cereal-based whiskies, including bourbon, rye, millet, oat and four-grain. All are matured in small new casks, so tend to be heavy on the vanilla side of things. Lovely packaging, though.

INDIANA

Midwest Grain Products Ingredients (MGP) Located near the Kentucky border, this power produces spirit for over 30 different bourbon, rye and corn whiskey brands. If you're not sure where your whisky was made... it's probably here.

IOWA

Cedar Ridge Distillery This winery makes Iowa Bourbon, Reserve Bourbon, Griff's Cowboy Whiskey, Short's Whiskey, a wheat whiskey, a malt whiskey and a white whiskey. Plans are afoot for a rye malt whiskey, too.

KENTUCKY

Alltech Lexington Brewing & Distilling Co. This brewery makes a malt whiskey, Pearse Lyons Reserve, and Town Branch Bourbon and Rye.

Barton Distillery aka Tom Moore (established in 1899) Kentucky's least-known distillery yet one of the most historic. Only one of its (many) brands is marketed outside of Kentucky: 1792 Ridgemont Reserve. If you're in Kentucky, get a hold of a bottle of VOB (Very Old Barton) – it's great!

Brown-Forman One of the founders of this incredibly successful distillery was George Garvin Brown, an influential figure in the history of bourbon. He released a version of their legendary Old Forester Bourbon in 1873. George Forman later joined and in 1890 the company became known as Brown-Forman. Today the distillery still makes Old Forester Bourbon and Early Times Whiskey. Old Forester uses a higher rye content mash bill than Early Times and is aged in new charred oak, whereas Early Times uses some refill casks. Interestingly, they use a 'thumper' instead of a 'doubler' for all distilling.

Buffalo Trace A distillery operation like no other, some 300 people work here. Their motto is 'Honour tradition, embrace change' and it's hard to argue that they don't live up to it; the master distiller can control the old column still from anywhere in the world using an app. The distillery runs five different mash bills to facilitate its remarkable 40-plus product list, you'll recognise popular brands such as W. L Weller, Sazerac Rye, Blanton's Eagle Rare and Pappy Van Winkle.

Corsair Distillery This distillery is marketing Triple Smoke, a malt whiskey; Wry Moon Unaged Rye Whiskey; Rasputin, a hopped whiskey; an early version of James E. Pepper Bourbon, Grainiac 9 Grain Bourbon.

Four Roses This brand was the top-selling bourbon in America when it was bought by Seagram in 1943. However, its reputation plummeted when Seagram began flogging a lower calibre blended whiskey in the same packaging. Now owned by The Kirin Brewery, the focus is once more on quality. The brewery makes use of five different proprietary yeast strains, including the original 'V', and two separate mash blends. The Four Roses Yellow Label (Original) is a complex blend of all 10 yeast/mash combinations.

Heaven Hill The largest independent and family-owned distillery in North America. Most famous for production of the Evan Williams and Elijah Craig brands of bourbon, among nearly 50 other bourbon, rye, and blended whiskey products.

Jim Beam The undisputed first family of bourbon can trace its lineage back 216 years, making it the oldest whiskey dynasty in the world. The huge distillery produces over a gallon of whiskey every second, much of which ends up in a Jim Beam White Label 4-year-old bottle. They also make Jim Beam Black (8-year-old),

Devil's Cut, Old Overholt Rye, Old Crow and Old Grandad. Small-batch bourbons include Knob Creek, Basil Hayden's and the most revered of them all, Booker's (named after Jim Beam's grandson).

Kentucky Bourbon Distillers Also known as Willet Distillers established in 1935. This family-owned distillery employs around 15 people and makes over 20 different bourbon and rye labels, most of which are revivals of long-gone pre-Prohibition brands.

Maker's Mark Famous for being really rather tasty, but perhaps even more famous for its wax-dripped bottle. In 2013, the brand announced plans to reduce the alcohol strength of the product from 45% to 42%; it was met with outrage from Maker's fans, causing Beam Inc. (the owner) to reconsider. Cynics consider the whole debacle to be an elaborate marketing exercise.

Old Pogue Distillery The original Old Pogue Distillery closed in the 1940s and the brand survived for years as an independent bottler. In 2012, the Pogue family opened a new distillery in Maysville, where they make Limestone Landing Rye and Five Fathers Rye.

Wild Turkey Most of the bourbons and rye whiskeys made at this Lawrenceburg distillery carry the Wild Turkey name, though they have recently begun to market Russell's Reserve as a separate brand. They also make Duke Bourbon.

Woodford Reserve Influential Scottish distiller James Christopher Crow worked here back in the 1830s, and the practices he established are still visible today with the use of three copper pot stills and red cypress wood fermenters, reminiscent of the Scottish washback. All the whiskey here is made using the nearby mineral-rich spring water, which Woodford credits with the floral aromatic taste of its products. I'd say it also has a lot to do with the triple-distillation process and high rye mash bill. The product range includes Woodford Reserve Bourbon, Woodford Reserve Double Oaked, a straight rye whiskey, straight malt whiskey and a wheat whiskey.

MARYLAND

Lyon Distilling Co. Maryland was once the fifth-biggest whiskey-producing state. This distillery makes Maryland Free State Rye, which is currently only available in unpaged form, but give it a little time…

MASSACHUSETTS

Bully Boy Distillery This distillery is named after an old workhorse that used to tend the farm of Will and Dave Willis. They make a white whiskey and an aged wheat whiskey.

Nashoba Distillery This winery-turned-distillery uses a combination of new oak and ex-wine casks to age its single malt whiskey for five years.

Ryan & Wood Distillery Makers of a few different distilled products, including a rye whiskey that was launched in 2011 and is made in a 600-litre (634-quart) alembic still with an attached rectifying column.

Triple Eight Distillery Cog in the machine that is the Nantucket Vineyard and Cisco Brewers, this distillery produces a 10-year-old single malt called 'Notch' (i.e. not Scotch.) They also bottle a bourbon called Nor'Easter, named for the storms that batter New England.

MICHIGAN

Grand Traverse Distillery With plenty of locally grown rye and perhaps the best cherries in North America, it's hardly surprising that these guys, who set up in 2007, make a great rye whiskey and a flavoured cherry whiskey too. They also bottle a 3-year-old bourbon.

Journeyman Distillery This organic distillery is constructed largely from salvaged materials, giving it a striking look. Some of its early products are salvaged, too, like Ravenswood Rye, the first batch of which was made at Koval in Chicago, with successive batches being made at Journeyman. They are also releasing a four-grain whiskey called Silver Cross, Featherbone Bourbon, Flat

Landers Bourbon, Buggy Whip Wheat Whiskey, Three Oaks Single Malt Whiskey and a wheat whiskey. Oh, and they have a bar there, too.

New Holland Brewing Co. This brewery-turned-distillery produces some bizarre whiskies, including Malthouse Brewers Whiskey, made from malted barley, smoked barley and rye; Barrel Hatter Royale, which is a hopped whiskey; and Beer Barrel Bourbon.

MISSOURI

Square One Distillery Another brewery-cum-distillery. Square One release spirits under the 'Spirit of St. Louis' brand, including J.J. Neukomm Whiskey, which is made from malt smoked with cherry wood and aged in Missouri oak casks.

NEVADA

Las Vegas Distillery Established in 2011 by a first-generation American Hungarian family from Transylvania, this small distillery makes 2-year-old Nevada 150 bourbon from local yellow corn. There are a few other products, too, including something called 'Rumskey'…

NEW MEXICO

Don Quixote Distillery Dr. Ron Dolin, the proprietor of this distillery, had a long career in engineering and is something of a tinkerer – he made a solar-powered still when he was just 19. Since establishing the distillery, Don has built (from scratch) no fewer than seven stills, which are apparently optimized to deal with the Jemez Mountains and the distillery's altitude of 2,225 metres (7,300 feet). The distillery makes blue-corn bourbon.

Santa Fe Spirits Established by Englishman Colin Keegan in 2010, this distillery has just released a single malt whiskey called (wait for it…) Colkegan. The whiskey is made from barley that has been smoked with mesquite and matured in a climate-controlled warehouse.

NEW YORK

Hillrock Estate Distillery Definitely one to watch. This distillery in the Hudson

Valley is not only floor-malting its own barley, but growing it on its own estate, too. Future releases aim to explore the estate's terroir. While it matures, they have released the only 'solera'-aged bourbon that I have ever come across.

Long Island Spirits Established in 2007, this distillery makes Pine Barrens Single Malt Whiskey and Rough Rider Bourbon, which would appear to be bought in and extra-matured in brandy casks.

Tuthilltown New York state's first whiskey distillery since 1919 is located on a farm in the Hudson Valley. It was set up in 2003 by Ralph Erenzo and here they make six types of whiskey under the Hudson brand, which was bought by William Grant in 2012. Interestingly, the warehouse is littered with speakers blasting out hip hop music with the aim of agitating the liquid to accelerate maturation. As ludicrous as this might sound, keeping the liquid moving slightly will help it permeate the wood.

Van Brunt Stillhouse This hipster distillery opened in April 2012 and has already released a rather tasty 9-month-old malt whiskey. And a bourbon. Their first rye-based endeavour launched as we went to press and there's a four-grain American Whiskey on the cards, too.

OHIO
John McCulloch Distillery Green River Whiskey is made here – a reincarnation of the popular pre-Prohibition John McCulloch brand, also known as 'the whiskey without a headache'.

Staley Mill Farm & Distillery Located on the site of a historic family-owned farmstead, this distillery was constructed in 2011 by an Amish crew and aims to capture the essence of Ohio's distilling tradition. Currently they source heirloom rye and corn varieties, but wheels have been set in motion to grow their future requirements on the farm itself.

OREGON
Clear Creek Distillery Maker of McCarthy's Oregon Single Malt, which

was released way back in the 1990s. It is a 3-year-old whiskey distilled from a wash of peated barley that is sourced from Scotland and fermented by the Widmer Brothers Brewery in Oregon. Oregon oak is used for maturation.

Edgefield Distillery A distillery on a golf course. Edgefield makes Hogshead Single Malt and a number of small-release whiskies under the Devil's Bit label. Currently they are all only available to buy at McMenamins entertainment spots.

House Spirits This one is on my 'one to watch list'. Current releases include the Westward malt whiskey, which is made from American barley, ale yeast and aged in new American oak casks.

Ransom Spirits For me, this distillery is better-known for its fantastic 'Old Tom' gin, but it also makes bourbon under the Henry DuYore's label, and Ransom Emerald 1865 Whiskey, an Irish-style whiskey made with rye, barley and oats to an original recipe from 1865.

Rogue Spirits Perhaps more famous for its beers, this field-to-glass brewer and distiller makes Rogue Dead Guy Whiskey, a four-grain whiskey and Chatoe Rogue Single Malt Whiskey.

Stein Distillery This farm-to-bottle distillery, grows its own rye and corn, which goes into Stein Straight Bourbon and rye.

PENNSYLVANIA
Mountain Laurel Spirits 'Live & Let Rye' craft producer of excellent rye whiskies, including a delicious vermouth cask-finished expression.

Pittsburgh Distilling Co. In 1794, Phillip Wigle defended his right to distil and tussled with a tax collector. He was hanged. In 2011, the Pittsburgh Distilling Co. (totally unrelated to Wigle) began releasing whiskey under the Wigle brand. It now makes rye and wheat whiskies.

RHODE ISLAND
Sons of Liberty Spirits Co. If death metal was a distillery... These guys use

beer as the focus and make Uprising Whiskey, a whiskey distilled from stout and aged in a combination of American oak and French oak; and Battle Cry single malt, distilled from a Belgian-style beer that has been fermented with Trappist yeast. They also release seasonal whiskies, one of which is hopped.

TENNESSEE

Corsair Distillery This distillery makes Triple Smoke, a malt whiskey; Wry Moon Unaged Rye Whiskey; Rasputin, a hopped whiskey; and they have plans for many other whiskies including an oatmeal stout and a chocolate mocha porter. They also distil the Collier & McKeel whiskey brand. This is their second distillery; the first is in Bowling Green, KY.

George Dickel The man himself, George Dickel, purchased Cascade Hollow distillery back in 1888–89. After George's death and the end of Prohibition, Schenley Group bought the distillery, hoping to cash in on Tennessee whiskey's official classification. Just like its top rival Jack Daniel's, George Dickel uses the Lincoln County Process but approaches it in a slightly different way by steeping the whiskey in charcoal pellets as opposed to dripping it through. The spirit is also chilled down to around 6°C/43°F before filtration to improve the clarity. The effect of this technique is apparent when comparing the potent aroma of Dickel's White Dog to the soft, buttery nuances of its No.1 Corn Whiskey.

Jack Daniel's The best-selling non-blended whiskey in the world, this global product is still produced in the tiny town of Lynchburg where Jack Daniel himself started distilling whiskey for sale in 1875. It was Jack's nephew and successor, Lemuel Motlow, who drove the business into the 20th century and he insisted on using a superior grade of corn, granting it a good reputation. After Motlow's death, his sons grew the business until its sale to Brown-Forman in 1956. Clever advertising campaigns propelled it to stardom by playing off the small-town, slow-paced lifestyle that the iconic black and white bottle still stands for. The smell of Jack's Old No.7 is unquestionably banoffee pie and barbecue, with pecans and pancake batter.

Prichard's Tennessee's first new distillery in 50 years was licensed in 1977. The operation is mostly housed in an old grade school with the classrooms, gymnasium and teacher's lounge made full use of. Its interesting portfolio of products includes a tasty Single Malt, aged in new 15-gallon white-oak casks in an attempt to accelerate the maturation process, a Double Chocolate Bourbon matured with the help of locally sourced cocoa nibs and a Tennessee Whiskey, unique among its peers because it isn't charcoal mellowed.

TEXAS

Balcones Refreshingly disruptive among the sanctioned archetypes of the whiskey world, Balcones was founded by Chip Tate in the small city of Waco in 2008. This award-winning experimental distillery has rapidly grown to become one of the largest in Texas. Their innovative range of products include two varieties of blue corn whiskey, the first Texan single malt, special-release bourbons and a smoked corn whiskey.

Garrison Brothers Distillery Progressive producer of Texan bourbon, they currently have a range of products with names that play nicely to the Texan stereotype, such as The Young Gun (young bourbon) and The Cowboy (barrel-strength bourbon).

UTAH

High West The world's first (and perhaps only) ski-in whiskey distillery is set on the Western edge of the Rocky Mountains. It's also the first to open in Utah since 1870. The distillery's original expression is the green and creamy Valley Tan, with the name being a nod to Mormon whiskey-producing pioneers of the region. The portfolio of High West also boats a serious selection of products whose components are brought in from other distilleries.

VERMONT

Silo Distillery This distillery produces a bourbon made from both corn and rye grown around the Connecticut River Valley of Vermont.

VIRGINIA

A. Smith Bowman Originally founded in 1934 and now owned by the Sazerac Company A. Smith Bowman redistils whiskey originally distilled at the Buffalo Trace Distillery (also owned by Sazerac) in Kentucky. It markets bourbon under the labels Virginia Gentleman, Bowman Brothers and John J. Bowman.

Catoctin Creek Distillery This Virginia distillery makes Roundstone Rye, which is available in 40%, 46% and barrel-proof (58%) strengths. Solar power accounts for 85% of the power used at Catoctin Creek.

Copper Fox Distillery Rick Wasmund took a six-week internship at Bowmore on Islay back in 2000; five years later he fired up the stills at the Copper Fox Distillery at the foot of the Blue Ridge Mountains in Sperryville, Virginia. The distillery malts its own barley and dries it with cherry and apple-wood smoke for Wasmund's single malt whiskey. Copper Fox Rye Whiskey is made from a mash of ⅓ malted barley and ⅔ Virginan Rye.

George Washington Distillery This distillery was founded in 1797 by President George Washington. He employed a Scotsman named James Anderson to build it, and two years later it was the largest distillery in North America. The distillery burned down in 1814, but a near-replica rebuilt in 2007. 1,000 bottles of the original recipe unaged rye whiskey were released in 2014 available to buy only at the distillery.

Reservoir Distillery Founded by Jay Carpenter and David Cuttino, this Richmond distillery makes bourbon, rye and wheat whiskey.

WASHINGTON

Bainbridge Distillers A USDA-certified organic island distillery that makes Bainbridge Battle Point Organic Whiskey, a whiskey made mostly from Washington white wheat and matured in 10-gallon American Oak barrels made by a family-run cooperage in Hot Springs, Arkansas.

Heritage Distilling Founded by Jennifer Stiefel, this distillery holds more trademarks than your average multinational corporation, including 'Your Whiskey, Your Way'™, 'My Batch'™, 'Cask Club'™ and 'Field to Flask'™. What does all this mean? Not a great deal, except for the fact that you can enrol in a DIY whiskey programme at the distillery. They currently make Elk Rider's blended whiskey and Commander's Rye, which is based on George Washington's Mount Vernon recipe.

Oola Distillery This craft distillery makes Waitsburg Bourbon, which is a blend of bourbon sourced from elsewhere and bourbon made at the distillery.

Woodinville Whiskey Co. 'Bigger Dreams, Smaller Batches'. Working with Dave Pickerell of Maker's Mark fame, this distillery makes Mashbill No. 9 Bourbon and 100% Rye.

WISCONSIN

45th Parallel Spirits At 45th Parallel, the corn, wheat and rye are all bought in from Strate Farm, which is just down the road and situated on the 45th Parallel itself (halfway between the North Pole and the Equator). The spent grain is trucked to another local farm as cattle feed. The distillery makes Border Bourbon and New Richmond Rye.

Yahara Bay Spirits Jack of all trades. These guys make Yahara Bay Whiskey, 'V Bourbon' Whiskey and a single malt. They also bottle Charred Oak Bourbon and rye for RJR Spirits and make Death's Door Whiskey for Death's Door Spirits.

The Rest of the World

ARGENTINA

La Alanza Argentina's first dedicated malt whisky distillery started making whisky in 2012 and is located in Patagonia. The owner, Pablo Tognetti, sources his barley locally and casks include ex-bourbon, PX and Malbec varieties.

AUSTRALIA

Bakery Hill These guys produce a small range of single malt whiskies, including a peated, unpeated and a double-matured whisky (finished in a Sherry cask). American oak casks are re-coopered in to 100-litre (106-quart) barrels, which coupled with the temperature of southern Australia, makes for a somewhat accelerated maturation process.

Black Gate New South Wales' first distillery was founded in 2012 and has supplemented its maturing malt stocks with a range of quick-to-market liqueur and vodka offerings. Whisky is matured in 100% Sherry casks.

Castle Glen Whiskey seems to be spelled with an 'e' here in Queensland, despite the Scottish distillery name. Wine and beer are also brewed, as well as absinthe, rum and a whole bunch of liqueurs. The first release was a 2-year-old in 2012.

Great Southern Distilling Company Very old port and Sherry casks, coupled with an unusually long fermentation (7–10 days) make GSDC an interesting one. Whisky is bottled under the Limeburners label, but they also bottle a bourbon-style whisky called Tiger Snake.

Hellyer's Road By far the biggest malt whisky distillery in Australia, with a single wash still that weighs in at 40,000 litres (42,500 quarts) – bigger than any in Scotland. Distillation is slow, so copper contact is significant (despite the bottom of the stills being made from steel), which is apparent in the light new-make spirit.

Nant On the site of an old water mill, the Nant Distillery in Tasmania conducted its first spirit runs in 2007. Get used to the name, as Keith Batt, the founder, plans on opening over 20 Nant whisky bars around the world over the coming years.

New World Whisky Distillery NWWD calls an old aircraft hanger its home. This distillery was founded in 2008 by David Vitale, a former Lark Distillery employee (Bill Lark helped him set up). The beautifully packaged 'Starward' is the distillery's first release, aged for roughly 4 years in ex-Sherry casks.

Old Hobart Formerly known as the Overeem Distillery, Bill Lark, from the nearby Lark Distillery, lends a hand here by processing all the mashing and fermenting to the exacting requirements of Old Hobart's owner, Casey Overeem. The Port Cask release from 2011 (60% ABV) was a beauty.

Lark Tasmania Distillery It might not seem like the obvious place for making malt whisky, but the mild climate, fresh air and diverse geography, not to mention plenty of peat, mean that Tasmania is not all that dissimilar to Scotland. The Sullivan's Cove whisky produced here won the prestigious World Whisky Awards 'Best Single Malt' award in 2014.

Timboon Railway Shed The Pilsner malt used here is sourced from the Red Duck microbrewery; the spirit matures in very small 20-litre (21-quart) casks that have been resized from larger barrels that previously held Tokaji wine and port, among other things.

William McHenry & Sons In 2011, McHenry left his sensible job in biotechnology and moved his family to Tasmania to set up a distillery. His 500-litre (528-quart) still is heated electrically and he holds the title of the most southerly whisky distillery in the world.

AUSTRIA

Whiskydestillerie J. Haider Austria's first whisky distillery was founded by Johann Haider in 1995 and released its first whisky in 1998. Austrian oak is used to mature the single malt, and a malt made from roasted barley, as well as a rye whisky is also produced here.

Reisetbauer Although this distillery was founded in 1994, they only began supplementing their fruit brandy offering at the end of the following year.

BELGIUM

Het Anker Brewer-cum-distiller, Charles Leclef, officially founded this distillery on his family's estate in 2010, although he had previously made the Gouden Carolus Single Malt back in 2008, which was distilled at a nearby genever distillery. Leclef uses an unhopped beer from his brewery as the wash.

The Owl The stills at this distillery were sourced from the demolished Caperdonich Distillery in Scotland, and it's these that are used to make The Belgian Owl, which was Belgium's first single malt when it launched in 2007.

BRAZIL

Union Distillery Long-time, large-scale producer of malt whisky. Most goes to blends, but they do also bottle a Brazilian single malt under the Union Club brand.

CANADA

Glenora Canada's first malt whisky distillery is modelled on the Scottish blueprint, even in its name. Glen Breton was their first (10-year-old) bottling back in 2000, but has been supplemented by numerous other expressions, including Glen Breton Ice, a 10-year-old aged in an ice wine barrel.

Hiram Walker Canada's most famous distillery was infact established by an American, Hiram Walker in 1858. Wary of the Temperance movement in the US, he built his distillery just across from the border near Windsor. This is the only distillery listed here to use malted rye instead of malted barley. The flavour of their Canadian Club owes much to the barrel blending method, which involves blending new makes of different characters, then vatting them together once matured to make new expressions.

Shelter Point Vancouver Island is home to a truly Scottish-style distillery. Shelter Point began distilling in 2011, but the final product aims to be a replica of some of the earliest Canadian grain distillates – this time fully matured. As with other subscribers to the new malt whisky revolution, they're into local sourcing here, even the stone and timber used to construct the distillery was cut nearby. The tall and narrow copper stills also add to the Scottish farmhouse effect. There are six different whiskies now available, and Shelter Point like to say that the sea air imparts nuances to every bottle.

Still Waters Located on the northern outskirts of Toronto, Still Waters is the brainchild of Barry Bernstein and Barry Stein, who started out as independent bottlers. Their current single malt bottlings are sourced from other Canadian distilleries while their own stuff matures.

CZECH REPUBLIC

Gold Cock Founded in 1877, Gold Cock is one of the oldest whisky distilleries in Europe outside of Ireland and Scotland. They make a 3-year-old blended whisky and a 12-year-old single malt.

DENMARK

Braunstein This micro-distillery produces both peated and unpeated whisky, the former being bought in from Port Ellen Matlings on Islay, no less. They have released a number of expressions since 2010, including whiskies finished in oloroso, Sherry and rum casks.

Fary Lochan Destilleri Hot off the bottling line, owner Jens Erik Jørgensen released his first 'lightly smoked' whisky in 2013, which partly comprises Danish malt that has been dried over a nettle fire.

Ørbæk Bryggeri The father-and-son team on the Danish island of Fyn operate both a brewery and a micro-distillery, which produces painfully small quantities of whisky under the Isle of Fionia label.

Stauning Self-sufficiency in tiny quantities, Stauning floor-malt their own Danish barley and dry some of it using

Danish peat, too. The four stills (two wash and two spirit) afford them an annual production of only 15,000 litres (15,850 quarts). A rye whisky is also made here.

ENGLAND

Adnams Copperhouse Long-famed for brewing, Adnams completed works on its distillery in 2010 and, with master distiller, John McCarthy, bottled its first whisky in 2013. Erring towards the American style, Adnams use a combination of column and pot as well as new oak for their single malt and three-grain whiskies.

St George's England's first whisky distillery for over 100 years is steaming ahead in terms of both its expressions and its sales, having topped over 100,000 bottles sales of both peated and unpeated whisky (bottled under the English Whisky Company label) in 2013.

FINLAND

Teerenpeli What started as a small whisky project for Anssi Pyysing in 2002, big enough only for the 3-year-old product to be sold in his restaurant, has now grown to a capacity of 30,000 litres (31,700 quarts) per year and includes a small range of lightly peated products.

FRANCE

Bertrand This Alsacian distillery, which started making whisky in 2002, buys its wash in from a local brewery and matures some of its whisky in casks that have previously held Banyuls wine. Around 7,000 bottles are produced annually in a town that has only 1,000 inhabitants.

Brasserie Michard Settled within that staple of the French wine and Cognac industry, Limousin, Michard use a proprietary yeast formula and released their first whisky in 2011.

Brûlerie du Revermont Distillers for hire they may be, but the use of stills designed to make perfume and 114-litre (120-quart) 'half-casks' at this Comté distillery make the Prohibition brand of whisky made here a rather unique proposition.

Brunet Currently Cognac's only whisky distillery, Brunet began bottling Tradition Malt in 2009 and also bottles under the Brenne brand in the USA.

Castan Producer of Villanova Berbie whisky, which will soon come in both peated and un-peated varieties from a third-generation mobile-still.

Claeyssens de Wambrechies One of France's oldest distilleries (dating back to 1817) was previously more famous for its liqueurs, but that changed in 2003 when they launched their first single malt, a 3-year-old. More recently a Wambrechies 12-year-old was released.

Distillerie de Northmaen Dominique Camus has been releasing 3-year-old whisky (under the Thor Boyo brand) from his craft brewery since 2005. Older releases are beginning to emerge, most recently an 8-year-old called Sleipnir.

Distillerie Gilbert Holl The tiny 150-litre/158-quart still used by Gilbert Holl was originally purchased in the early-1980s to make fruit brandy. In 2000, Holl began distilling whisky, but bottles are very few-and-far-between.

Domaine de Hautes-Glaces Perhaps France's most exciting new whisky distillery, the founders of this purpose-built operation, Jérémey Bricka and Frédéric Revol, intend on keeping almost every stage of their malt whisky and rye whisky production in-house, from malting right through to bottling. The first 3-year-old bottlings were released in 2015.

Glann ar Mor A recreation of traditional Scottish distillery can be found in Pleubian in Glann ar Mor. The distillery practises direct firing of its copper stills, and uses cold worm-tubs to condense. Two labels are available, the unpeated Glann ar Mor and the peated Kornog.

Grallet Dupic This distillery was founded in 1860, but whisky production only began years later after the owner, Hubert Grallet, accepted a drunken dare. They now produce peated and unpeated under the G. Rozelieures brand.

Hepp Uberach's 'other' distillery (Bertrand being the rival) produces a trio of single cask whiskies under the AWA (Authentic Whisky Alsace) label, which are finished in noble grape casks (riesling, gerwurtztraminer, pinot gris) and a non-age-statement whisky called Tharcis Hepp.

Lehmann The whisky made here (since 2000) is matured exclusively in French white wine casks. We have already seen Bordeaux and Sauternes being used to good effect, Coteaux-du-Layon is next to get the Lehmann treatment.

Meyer Originally a fruit eau de vie distillery, the 60-year-old Meyer distillery turned its hand to whisky in 2007 and now produces many of the own-label supermarket French malts and blends.

Warenghem This distillery was founded in 1900 by Leon Warenghem, but only released France's first single malt whisky in 1988. Warenghem continue to market a range of malts under the Armorik label, which range from 4 to 11 years in age.

GERMANY

Blaue Maus (Blue Mouse) This German distillery looks like a new-build home from the outside and that's because it's a new home for an old distillery. Blaue Maus was established in 1980 and now produces about ten single malts, most of which are matured in German oak.

Hammerschmiede The malt whisky made here (bottled under the Glen Iarran and Glen Els labels) was originally an ancillary product to a great range of bitters and liqueurs, but it is quickly taking precedent as sales grow. The distillery has become famous for its exploration into the journey of production, having released identical expressions with subtle shifts in wood smoke and cask finishing; these form the Journey and Ember range of releases.

Preussische Whiskydestillerie A 3-year-old whisky was released by this distillery in 2012, followed by three more in 2013. It is unique in its 6x distillation process and use of organic barley.

Slyrs Bavaria seems like a fitting place for whisky distillery given the association that the area has with beer. Slyrs celebrates this – the malt here is smoked with beech and matured in new US oak. I can highly recommend the PX-finished expression.

Stickum Brennerei This brewery in Düsseldorf, like many others, turned its attention to whisky-making in 2007. Distillation is conducted in a copper column still and maturation in various types of new and seasoned oak.

Sylter Not exactly a distillery, but an interesting anomaly nonetheless. The whisky bottled as Sylter Offshore is actually distilled at the Dolleruper Distillery in Dollerup, then shipped to the northern German island of Sylt for maturation, with the aim of imparting a marine character into the whisky.

INDIA

Amrut Malt whisky has been distilled here since the mid-1980s, and the distillery was originally founded in 1948. Indian barley is used for the unpeated variants, which is malted in Jaipur and New Delhi. There is quite a large range of expressions, with the 8-year-old Greed Angels being the oldest to date; evaporative losses over a long time in the Indian heat meant that only one-quarter of the contents of the cask survived.

McDowell's Originally established by a Scotsman, Angus McDowell in 1826. This distillery has come a long way since then, and now makes up a large chunk of the United Spirits portfolio, which sells over 130 million cases a year. A mere 1.5% of those cases hold malt whisky, distilled in Goa and aged for 3–4 years.

Paul John A diamond in the rough of the Indian whisky market, Paul John was founded in 1992 and quickly grew to be a leading spirit company. Indian malt is used at their distillery in Goa to make the single malt whisky. Scottish peat is used for their Scottish expression and peated malt in the 'Edited' expression. A climate-controlled underground warehouse is used to lessen the effects of fluctuating temperature and humidity during the five-year aging process.

IRELAND

Carlow This distillery operation in Bagenalstown is currently nameless, but was formed through a partnership between The Carlow Brewing Company in Ireland and Alltech, an agricultural manufacturer from the US. Alltech also owns the Lexington Distillery in Kentucky, and are now branching out to this new venture, with stills made in Kentucky, promises to be an Irish/American hybrid. First bottlings of a single malt were released in 2015.

Cooley John Teeling founded the Cooley distillery in 1987. This independent distillery went on to produce a range of different blended and single malt whiskies for a portfolio of clients. More recently the distillery has passed on to Beam Inc. for a rumoured $95 million (£56 million). Word on the street is that independent labels will soon cease production as Beam concentrate on their own brands.

Dingle An independent family-owned business that only came into being in 2012 and released its first whiskey in December 2015, this distillery makes whiskey, gin and vodka. Eschewing high-volume production in favour of artisanal methods, their whiskey is small batch and distilled in three distinctive handmade copper pot stills. One to watch for sure.

Kilbeggan This much older brother of the Cooley Distillery was brought back from extinction by John Teeling in 2007, exactly 250 years after it was originally built. One of the only wooden mash tuns in the world is still used at Kilbeggan along with stills that pre-date most of the distilleries in this book. Kilbeggan is also now owned by Beam Inc.

Midleton This large-scale operation is the result of Cork Distillery Group merging with John Power & Son and John Jameson & Son to form the Irish Distillers Group in 1966. The new Midleton distillery in Cork was built in 1975. The recently updated state-of-the-art site now makes dozens of expressions for brands like Jameson, Redbreast, Green Spot and Yellow Spot, using a range of corn, barley and malted barley and combinations of triple pot and column stills. The site houses what is thought to be the largest inactive pot still in the world at 143,000 litres (151,000 quarts).

Teeling Producing whiskey has been in the Teeling family since 1782 when Walter Teeling opened a craft distillery in the heart of Dublin, which was later purchased by Jameson. Two decades later, his descendent John Teeling founded the Cooley Distillery. 2015 saw the dawn of a new legacy of Teeling whiskey, with brothers Jack and Stephen opening the first new distillery in Dublin for 25 years in an area that was once a hub of whisky production. The new Teeling Distillery has so far picked up a string of awards and the future looks bright for them.

ITALY

Puni Destillerie The Ebensperger family founded Italy's first malt whisky distillery in 2012 and are now producing spirit from barley as well as malted wheat and rye. Stocks mature in ex-World War II bunkers and the first legal whiskies went on sale in 2015. The family have also released Puni Alba, which is a 1-year-old expression matured in Marsala casks.

JAPAN

Chichibu Founded in 2008 by Ichiro Akuto, this small distillery has gained a cult following of whisky geeks the world over. Their hands-on approach and commitment to the craft is evident, from malting their own barley to milling their grains in a specific way, to using casks and washbacks made out of Japanese mizunara oak. It seems that applying Japanese twists to Scottish malt whisky tradition results in some seriously sought-after expressions.

Fuji Gotemba Surprisingly, this is Japan's biggest distillery, producing over 12,000,000 litres (12,680,000 quarts) a year including grain whisky. It's American oak only here, however, and only a handful of the range of whiskies made here actually advertise it, including Fujisanroku 18-year-old.

Hakushu This brewery is set in lush forest on the slopes of Mount Kaikoma, and the thawed snow from the mountain is used to make the whisky here. The distillery seems to have drawn upon the themes of its tranquil surroundings to produce green, light, fresh and lucid products. The three-day fermentation process also helps with this, making it grassy and fruity. Opened in 1973, Hakushu was the biggest malt whisky distillery in the world back in the 1980s.

Miyagyiko A fairer touch when compared to its more northerly Nikka brother. In the 1960s Masataka Taketsuru apparently spent three years hunting down the site of this second distillery before he settled on the humid and peaceful area in the Miyagi Prefecture. Check out the Coffey grain release, which is all pencil shavings, caraway and menthol.

Shinshu With production hitting only 25,000 litres (26,500 quarts) a year, Shinshu is Japan's smallest active whisky distillery. After a few recent World Whisky Award wins, this little operation is fast becoming famous for its Mars Maltage blended malt.

White Oak Japan's second smallest distillery (60,000 litres/63,000 quarts a year) also happens to be its oldest. Their Akashi 15-year-old, which was released in 2013, is matured in konara oak, a relative of the better known mizunara.

Yamazaki Japan's first whisky distillery was built by Shinjiro Torii in 1923 on the outskirts of Kyoto. Now owned by Suntory (who also own Hakushu), it's the largest malt distillery in the country. Here diversity is important to Suntory, from the two types of barley used, to the eclectic family of mismatched pot stills, to the wide selection of casks for aging. The aim being to create unique compositions from a broad palette of flavours.

Yoichi Coal-fired stills and a traditional approach define the rugged style of Nikka's first distillery, which was founded by Masataka Taketsuru in the 1930s. The distillery is located on the Northern island of Hokkaido, chosen for its similarities to the Scottish Highlands.

LIECHTENSTEIN

Brennerei Telser An unconventional location for a malt distillery it certainly is, but this fourth-generation family-owned distillery relies heavily on tradition. The tiny pot stills (120 litres/127 quarts and 150 litres/158 quarts) here are wood fired after an epic 10-day fermentation (one of the longest I have come across). The spirit is subsequently matured in a 500-year-old cellar, exclusively in ex-pinot noir barrels.

THE NETHERLANDS

Us Heit The first Dutch whisky was bottled at the Us Heit brewery/distillery in 2005, made from locally grown barley malted at the brewery itself using a proprietary technique.

Zuidam Since 2007, this distillery in Holland has been bottling rye and malt whiskies. The current range includes a 5-year-old malt that comes in both peated and unpeated flavours, a 10-year-old matured in new American white oak and a 10-year-old matured in ex-Sherry casks. Zuidam rye has proven itself especially popular amongst bartenders.

NEW ZEALAND

NZ Malt Whisky Co. Investors have piled in on this operation which will no doubt prove to be formidable. Older stocks inherited from the decommissioned Wilsons Willowbank Distillery in Dunedin have also been bottled under various labels, including Milford, South Island, Diggers & Ditch (a blended malt), and Water of Leith (a blend).

NORTHERN IRELAND

Bushmill's Often credited as the oldest distillery in the world, Diageo, Bushmill's current owners, date its history back to 1608. This may be a stretch, but even at the more realistic approximation of 1784, it's still impressively old. Ten stills and a production capacity of 4.5 million litres (4.75 million quarts) a year affords Bushmill's a wide variety of products, including Black Bush and Bushmill's Original blends, a 10-year-old malt and older malts including a 16-year-old (finished in port pipes) and a 21-year-old (finished in Madeira casks).

NORWAY

Agder Brenneri Norway's first single malt whisky is produced at the Agder Brenneri Distillery. Current annual release quota is just 1,750 bottles of 3-year-old whisky, which has been matured in a single ex-Sherry butt.

PAKISTAN

Murree Brewery Founded 150 years ago, the Murree brewery supplied beer to the British colonies. Now they make a few single malt expressions, too, among many other things. A cooler climate than India means that maturation can be drawn out a little longer. A 12-year-old and 18-year-old make up the core range.

SOUTH AFRICA

Drayman's This brewery in Pretoria is somewhat of a hidden gem. Their malt whisky production involves a ten-day fermentation process and maturation in French oak casks that have previously held red South African wine. The distillery's bottles under the label 'Drayman's Highveld Single Malt'.

James Sedgwick Despite a 25-year history of whisky production, it's sporadic malt whisky releases that seem to have defined this grain/malt distillery over the past decade, but their 10-year-old – matured in ex-bourbon casks was released in 2015 (after a 3-year wait).

SPAIN

Destilerias Liber Founded in 2001, the smaller of the two Spanish whisky-makers produce a range of spirit categories, inducing a 5-year-old single malt whisky called Embrujo de Granada.

Distilerio Molino del Arco Surprisingly, whisky distilling started here in 1962,

making Molino del Arco one of the oldest European producers outside of the British Isles. Grain and malt whiskies are made here, with combined production capacity topping 10 million litres (10.6 million quarts) per year. The distillery includes its own maltings too and produces a range of blended and malt whiskies, including a newly released 10-year-old.

SWEDEN

Gammelstilla Handmade and custom designed stills are the order of the day in this new Swedish distillery, which began running spirits in 2012. First bottles were released in 2016.

Gotland Production began at Gotland in May 2012 with a couple of unique talking points. Firstly, all the barley used for their malt whisky is local and organic, malted on-site, and turned by their own custom made 'malt-bot'. Secondly, their ageing warehouse is underground, meaning that temperature and humidity are more constant.

Grythyttan Set on an 800-year-old farm, this distillery also has around 800 shareholders. A cask-strength 3-year-old was the first official whisky release at the tail end of 2013.

High Coast Distillery (formerly Box) Founded in 2005 by Mats and Per de Vahl, High Coast are pioneers of the exciting Swedish distilling movement. 'Made for whisky geeks, by whisky geeks' ought to be their tagline, as every stage of the production process has been meticulously researched. Their earlier 'educational' releases demonstrate how different decisions impact the flavour of the final product and their most recent 'Origins' series is a tribute to their heritage and the dramatic landscape of the High Coast.

Mackmyra Sporting an innovative gravity-fed system, contained within its 37-metre (121-feet) high chassis, Mackmyra's new distillery (to replace the site founded in 1999) began production in 2012. Two styles of whisky are made here, one fruity and the other smoky – derived from burnt juniper wood and bog moss.

Norrtelje Brenneri Oloroso and ex-apple brandy casks are on the menu at Stockholm's nearest distillery located on a fifth generation family-owned farm.

Smögen Full-bodied and smoky is the aim for Pär Caldenby's new distillery, which began spirit runs in 2010. Caldenby is a whisky author himself and personally designed and sourced the materials used to construct the distillery. Their first whisky, a cask-strength bottling called Primör, was released in 2014.

Spirit of Hven There's a long list of obsessive goings-on at Henric Molin's distillery in the Island of Hven. The wood policy is extremely regimented, with oak being sourced from the USA, Spain and Japan, before lengthy drying periods and seasoning. Some barley is peated, sometimes burnt with seaweed and seagrass. Then there's the oak laboratory, which completed construction in 2013 and promises to be the go-to facility for research into oaks effect on spirits.

SWITZERLAND

Bauernhofbrennerei Lüthy After four years of whisky production, a floor malting was built at Lüthy in 2009, which now produces the Swiss peated malt requirements for the distillery.

Hollen Purpose-built in 1999, Hollen Whisky Distillery produced the first Swiss single malt. Like most Swiss distilleries, they use a mixture of French red and white wine casks. 4-year-old and 5-year-old expressions are available.

Langatun Producers of Old Dear (unpeated) and Old Bear (peated) single malt whiskies, which are both matured for 5 years exclusively in Swiss and French oak. They also produce a single barrel rye whisky, called Old Eagle.

Brauerei Locher This brewery was founded in 1886 and recently turned its hands to distilling. Among its repertoire is the practice of using very old beer casks to mature its whisky, but wine and bourbon casks are used, too. Peated and unpeated expressions are available.

Brennerei Stadelmann This distillery was, for 70 years, one of many nomad operations that could be mobilised if the distiller desired. It finally settled down in 2000 under the guidance of the founder's grandson, Hans Stadelmann. A 3-year-old became the first official bottling in 2011.

Whisky Castle Perhaps Swizerland's best known dedicated whisky distillery produces a mere 10,000 litres (10,565 quarts) of alcohol a year, making it smaller than any in Scotland. But they make up for it in variety, having released a range of young expressions since 2004.

TAIWAN

Yuan Shan Distillery Producers of the Kavalan brand of Taiwanese whisky, Yuan Shan is perhaps the most visited distillery in the world, attracting over 3,000 visits a day. Casks here are tied together in groups of 4 to stop them rolling during earthquakes, and with over a dozen expressions there are many to protect.

WALES

Penderyn In the year 2000, the Welsh Whisky Companies distillery began producing the first Welsh whisky in over 94 years in the foothills of the Brecon Beacons. Their two-stage pot and column still set-up is unique as it does the job in one single distillation. Other complexities in the design mean there is a lot of reflux in the still, resulting in a high ABV spirit of 86–92%, with fruity and floral notes. It's the cleanliness of the spirit that opens it up to the huge influence of wood. Their 10-year-old – matured in ex-bourbon casks – is due in 2015 (after a 3-year wait).

INDEX

Tristan Stephenson is an award-winning bar operator, bartender, barista, chef, some-time journalist and the bestselling author of *The Curious Bartender* series of drinks books. In 2009 he was ranked 3rd in the UK Barista Championships. He was then awarded UK bartender of the year in 2012, and in the same year was included in *London Evening Standard*'s annual round up of the 'Top 1000 most influential Londoners'.

After intially launching his career working in various restaurant kitchens in his native Cornwall (on the South West coast of England), in 2007 Tristan was given the opportunity to design cocktails and run bar operations at chef Jamie Oliver's Fifteen. He went on from there to work for the world's biggest premium drinks company, Diageo, and then to co-found Fluid Movement with Thomas Aske (a fellow former drinks industry brand ambassador) in 2009. Their globally renowned drinks consultancy has been the brains behind the drinks programmes at some of the world's top drinking and eating destinations. Fluid Movement then went on to open their own bars in London – Purl, in 2010, and then the highly successful Worship Street Whistling Shop in 2011. (The Whistling Shop was named by *Time Out* as 'London's Best New Bar' in 2011 and was placed in the 'World's Fifty Best Bars' for three consecutive years.)

In 2014 Tristan and Thomas opened their next venue together. Surfside, a family-friendly steak and lobster restaurant on Polzeath beach, this time back in Tristan's native Cornwall. The restaurant was awarded the No. 1 Position in *The Sunday Times*'s newspapers 'Best alfresco dining spots in the UK 2015.' Tristan himself served as head chef there for the first summer and continues to closely manage the food and beverage menu. Surfside has since become a well-established and a popular part of the Cornwall summer and surfing scene.

In 2016 Fluid Movement opened a small hotel with no less than three more London bars, all at the same site in fashionable Shoreditch in the East End of London. The hotel, The Napoleon, was unique in that it had just one bedroom! And the bars (all of which provided room service...) were The Devil's Darling (a classic cocktail bar), Sack (a sherry and tapas bar), and most significantly, Black Rock (a bar dedicated to whisky). Significantly, because Black Rock has won *Time Out*'s 'UK's Best Specialist Bar' for three years consecutively (from 2017–2019). The original intimate basement space has since expanded to also include the first-floor Black Rock Tavern, styled after the izakayas of Japan, and offering whisky highballs, draught beers and a curated collection of malts, bourbons and ryes from around the world. A second Black Rock site opened in Bristol in the Summer of 2019 and further bar openings are planned across the UK.

Tristan's writing debut, *The Curious Bartender Volume I: The Artistry & Alchemy of Creating the Perfect Cocktail* was published in 2013 and shortlisted for the prestigious André Simon Award for excellence in food and drink writing. His second book, *The Curious Bartender: An Odyssey of Malt, Bourbon & Rye Whiskies* (from which this book is abridged) hit the bookshelves in 2014. In 2015 he published *The Curious Barista's Guide to Coffee* (his credentials as a barista as well as a bartender coming into play) and he had, in addition, harvested, processed, roasted and brewed the first cup of UK-grown coffee from the Eden Project in Cornwall.

In 2016 his fourth book, in what was by now an established series, *The Curious Bartender's Gin Palace*, was again shortlisted for the André Simon and took readers on a tour of the most exciting gin distilleries the world has to offer. His fifth book, *The Curious Bartender's Rum Revolution*, appeared in 2017 and demonstrated how rum has moved beyond its Caribbean heartlands, with new distilleries appearing in Brazil, Venezuela, Colombia and Guatemala and in very unexpected places, such as Australia, Japan, Mauritius and the Netherlands. His sixth title, *The Curious Bartender Volume 2: The New Testament*, (an eagerly anticipated follow-up to the original bestselling *Curious Bartender Volume 1*) was met with great enthusiasm by his worldwide bartending fanbase upon publication in 2018. Once again it featured classic cocktail recipes plus Tristan's own highly imaginative spins and in-depth explanation of classic drinks and modern mixology methods.

Then in 2019 Tristan brought the growing number of American whiskey and bourbon collectors and fans *The Curious Bartender's Whiskey Road Trip*. This coast-to-coast tour of the most exciting whiskey distilleries in the US, 'from small-scale craft operations to the behemoths of bourbon', is surely one of Tristan's most impressive and ambitious works to date.

Finally, Tristan's other commercial enterprises include his drinks brand Aske-Stephenson (again with business partner Fluide Movement's Thomas Aske) which manufactures and sells pre-bottled cocktails in flavours as diverse as Rhubarb & Custard Negroni, Bramble Garden, Peanut Butter & Jam Old-fashioned, Sesame & Popcorn Daiquiri and Flat White Russian. He has also launched an on-line whisky subscription service, whisky-me.com, offering top-quality single malt whiskies for home delivery. In addition, in March 2017 Tristan joined the supermarket chain Lidl UK as a consultant on their highly-regarded own-brand spirits range.

Tristan travels extensively for work but lives in Cornwall and is husband to Laura and father to two small children. In his very limited spare time he runs, rides a Triumph motorcycle, takes photos, designs websites, bakes stuff, cooks a lot, reads avidly, attempts various DIY tasks beyond his level of ability and collects whiskey and books.

❯❯❯ ACKNOWLEDGMENTS ❮❮❮

Writing the original unabridged book *The Curious Bartender: An Odyssey of Malt, Bourbon & Rye Whiskies* (from which this smaller volume is extracted) in only nine months was not an easy task and would certainly not have been possible without the help and support of a small group of individuals – this book is dedicated to you.

Addie Chinn, for the continued development of our symbiotic photo-lingual relationship. Craig Harper, for regular words of support, and for completing a lap of Scotland in four-days. Daryl Haldane, for bringing Orkney to life (and bringing life to Orkney), fact-checking and long conversations about wood. Itoh Takuya and Rogerio Igarashi for handling everything on the Japan leg of the tour and being generally amazing hosts. Thanks also to the hundreds of brand ambassadors, distillery managers, mashmen, cask-fillers, bottle-cappers and distillery cleaners who have made each and very trip an experience to treasure. You're too numerous a group to list, but know who you are. Thanks to the team at RPS – especially Nathan Joyce – who I think (like me) got a lot more than they bargained for with this one!

Finally, thanks to my wife and son (who has been joined by a little sister since the original volume was written) for their patience, endurance, and love throughout the long months and late nights of research and writing.